Globalization and the Good

To my parents, David and Anne,

who first introduced me to

beauty, truth and goodness

Globalization and the Good

Edited by Peter Heslam

WILLIAM B. EERDMANS PUBLISHING COMPANY
GRAND RAPIDS, MICHIGAN / CAMBRIDGE U.K.

Originally published 2004 in Great Britain by
Society for Promoting Christian Knowledge
Holy Trinity Church
Marylebone Road
London NW1 4DU

This edition published 2004 in the United States of America by
Wm. B. Eerdmans Publishing Company
255 Jefferson Ave. S.E., Grand Rapids, Michigan 49503 /
P.O. Box 163, Cambridge CB3 9PU, U.K.
www.eerdmans.com

Manufactured in Great Britain

06 05 04 03 02   5 4 3 2 1

ISBN 0-8028-2845-0

Contents

The Contributors

Timothy Gorringe is St Luke's Professor of Theological Studies at the University of Exeter. Previously he was Chaplain and Fellow at St John's College, Oxford. He has published widely, including *Capital and the Kingdom: Theological Ethics and Economic Order* (Orbis, 1994), *Fair Shares: Ethics and the Global Economy* (Thames & Hudson, 1999) and *A Theology of the Built Environment* (Cambridge University Press, 2002).

Brian Griffiths taught at the London School of Economics and Political Science before becoming Professor of Banking and International Finance at the City University and a Director of the Bank of England. From 1985 to 1990 he served as Head of Margaret Thatcher's Policy Unit. In this role he was responsible for domestic policy-making and was one of the chief architects of the government privatization and deregulation programmes. On leaving No. 10 he was made a member of the House of Lords and became Vice-Chairman of Goldman Sachs International. He is also a non-executive director of several companies, including Times Newspaper Holdings and ServiceMaster. He has written and lectured extensively on economic issues and on the relationship of Christian faith to politics, business and finance.

David Held is Graham Wallas Professor of Political Science at the London School of Economics and Political Science. Among his recent books are *Globalization/Anti-Globalization* (Polity, 2002), *Global Transformations* (Polity, 1999) and *Democracy and the Global Order* (Polity, 1995).

Peter Heslam is Director of the Capitalism Project and Lecturer in Social and Economic Ethics at the London Institute for Contemporary Christianity and a Tutor at Ridley Hall in

Cambridge. Previously he was a Director of Studies in the Cambridge Theological Federation. He is also Convenor of JustShare, a consortium of agencies and denominations that engages at senior business and government level with the ethics of economic globalization. He represents the Archbishop of Canterbury on this issue at the World Council of Churches and the Anglican Consultative Council. He has published widely, including *Creating a Christian Worldview* (Eerdmans, 1998) and *Globalization: Unravelling the New Capitalism* (Grove, 2002). He is a Senior Research Associate of the Von Hügel Institute, St Edmund's College, Cambridge.

Clive Mather is Chairman of Shell UK and was Head of Global Learning in Shell International in 2002. He is also Chairman of the Government/Industry Steering Group on Corporate Social Responsibility, Chairman of Lensbury Limited and Deputy Chairman of the Windsor Leadership Trust. He writes and speaks on leadership and learning internationally, drawing on a wide variety of experiences in different functions and countries.

Cynthia Moe-Lobeda teaches Christian ethics at Seattle University. She has served as Director of the Washington DC office of the Center for Global Education, and as a missionary/health worker in Honduras. Moe-Lobeda is author of *Healing a Broken World: Globalization and God* (Fortress, 2002) and co-author of *Saint Francis and the Foolishness of God* (Orbis, 1993) and *Say to this Mountain: Mark's Story of Discipleship* (Orbis, 1996). Her forthcoming book, with Fortress Press, concerns the role of the Church in public life. She lectures and consults internationally in the area of theology and ethics.

Ann Pettifor is Director of Jubilee Research at the New Economics Foundation (NEF), a leading economics think-tank based in London. In this role she leads NEF's work on international finance and has edited *Real World Economic Outlook: The Legacy of Globalization* (Macmillan, 2003). This is an annual report shadowing the IMF's *World Economic Outlook*. In 1996 she co-founded the Jubilee 2000 campaign for the cancellation of poor country debts, and was its director for five years. She is on the board of the United Nations' Human Development Report. She holds a degree in English from Witswatersrand University, Johannesburg, and an honorary doctorate from the University of Newcastle.

Michael Schluter is the founder and Chairman of the Jubilee Centre, a Christian research organization based in Cambridge. He is also Chairman of the Keep Sunday Special Campaign and the Relationships Foundation. He has a PhD in agricultural economics from Cornell University and worked in East Africa for six years as a consultant for the World Bank and the International Food Policy Research Institute. He co-authored *The R Factor* (1993) and *The R Option* (2003) and contributed to *Relational Justice* (1994), *Building a Relational Society: New Priorities for Public Policy* (1996) and *Christian Perspectives on Law and Relationism* (2000).

Michael Taylor is currently Professor of Social Theology in the University of Birmingham and Director of the World Faiths Development Dialogue. Previously he was Principal of the Northern Baptist College, Lecturer in Ethics and Theology at Manchester University, Director of Christian Aid, President of the Jubilee 2000 UK Debt Coalition and President and Chief Executive of the Selly Oak Colleges in Birmingham. He is the author of numerous books and articles, the most recent of which is *Christianity, Poverty and Wealth: The Findings of Project 21* (SPCK, 2003).

Jim Wallis is Executive Director and Editor of *Sojourners* and Convener of Call to Renewal. He is a leading international commentator on ethics and public life and a spokesperson for faith-based initiatives to overcome poverty. In great demand as a public speaker, he is featured frequently on TV and radio, and his columns appear in the major US broadsheets. He also lectures at Harvard University's Kennedy School of Government on 'Faith, Politics, and Society'. *Time* magazine named Wallis one of the '50 Faces for America's Future'. His books include *Faith Works* (SPCK, 2000), *The Soul of Politics*

(New Press, 1994) and *Who Speaks for God? A New Politics of Compassion, Community, and Civility* (Bantam Dell, 1996).

Michael Woolcock is a senior social scientist with the Development Research Group at the World Bank, and an Adjunct Lecturer in Public Policy at Harvard University's Kennedy School of Government. His research uses interdisciplinary theories and methods to address two major themes: social institutions and political economy. He is currently completing a book on social capital and economic development and is co-editing a book on incorporating social capital issues into the design and evaluation of large development projects. He has spoken extensively on the social dimensions of development theory, research and policy, to diverse audiences in over 20 countries and was an author of the World Bank's *World Development Report 2000/01* on poverty, and a contributor to its recent *Policy Research Report on Globalization, Growth, and Poverty*.

Acknowledgements

My first word of thanks must go to Mark Greene and my other colleagues on the staff and board of the London Institute for Contemporary Christianity, together with the Capitalism Project Partners. Without their support of my involvement in this volume and their confidence in the value of the final product, this book would never have seen the light of day. My voluntary research assistant, Jeff Jordan, and my proofreaders, Eunice Burton and Katy Coutts, deserve special thanks for their help in preparing the manuscript for publication.

Second, I am deeply grateful to the contributors to this volume. They produced the papers which make up the various chapters in the midst of busy and demanding schedules. In so doing they have put a lot of themselves into their writing; they have allowed their contributions to reflect their own particular vocation, commitments and sphere of work. Indeed, their personal dedication to engaging with economic globalization as an issue of overriding moral importance has been a great stimulus to me and has sustained me through the more tedious aspects of editing text.

Third, I wish to thank most warmly my colleagues in JustShare, who helped to provide the context from which four of the chapters derive. From its inception in the autumn of 2002, JustShare has been one of the great adventures of my working life. Together we have studied, discussed and written about the key issues of global economic justice. We have listened both to the beneficiaries of globalization and to its victims. Above all we have strategized, organized, mobilized and taken action. This experience has taught me that the ambiguities and complexities of globalization can serve to create and energize; they are not bound to overwhelm and paralyse. The project has demanded more faith and courage than I suspect any of us anticipated, but it has borne more fruit than we ever imagined. I am truly grateful for such committed and indefatigable colleagues.

Next I wish to thank my many friends in the worlds of economics, business and banking who first drew my attention to the importance of this issue. It has been my regular meetings with them that have done so much to clarify my thinking and have kept me rooted in the economic realities of contemporary business practice. It has been a great encouragement to see so many of them taking a stand for ethical principles in the context of a highly competitive and rapidly changing business environment. This has underscored my conviction that moral leadership is as much the preserve of business as it is of every other sphere of society, including those often associated with 'moral communities'.

Last, I offer my greatest thanks to the fellow members of my household: Judith, Samuel, Benjamin and Julia. Their love, cheerfulness and fortitude have provided a constant source of inspiration and ample reason for much gratitude and celebration.

Peter Somers Heslam
Cambridge, Lent 2004

Let us choose to unite the power of markets with the authority of universal ideals. Let us choose to reconcile the creative forces of private entrepreneurship with the needs of the disadvantaged and the requirements of future generations.

Kofi Annan

Introduction

PETER HESLAM

The debate about economic globalization is still in its infancy. Economists and scientists produce fresh studies on its negative impacts on poverty and the environment. Politicians and activists disseminate the data. The business lobby and consumer groups respond in defensive mode and seek to prove their social and ecological credentials. Newspapers and other media cover the controversy, serve to intensify it and reach a variety of conclusions. The general public, burdened as they are by a host of consumer concerns, become confused and bewildered. Governments are left paralysed, unwilling or unable to take sufficiently decisive action.

The truth is that contemporary economic globalization is a highly complex phenomenon, full of apparently contradictory trends. It can help to raise living and environmental standards for significant numbers of people at the same time as it helps to widen the gap between rich and poor and increases the destruction and depletion of natural resources. This reflects the fact that it is perfectly possible to achieve a good in some areas at the cost of creating a bad elsewhere. The challenge, therefore, is to shun the media-fostered mindset that only understands polarities, to consider all sides of the issue, and to base judgements on as full an account of the available evidence as possible. Genuine solutions can only be found by seeking to understand the problems and opportunities in their complexity and interconnectedness.

This involves creating space for perspectives that reflect religious and moral starting-points. Such starting-points have proven deeply influential in giving shape both to the globalization agenda and to responses to it. For this reason, if for no other, they cannot be dismissed as irrelevant or outmoded. This book is an attempt to open up some of these perspectives, for the purpose of increasing understanding and moving on the debate. As such it serves as a sequel to my *Globalization: Unravelling the New Capitalism* (Grove, 2002), which is an attempt to describe the phenomenon of economic globalization, to outline an ethical perspective on it informed by Christian tradition, and to suggest guidelines to ensure that globalization works as a blessing rather than as a curse for the poor and the natural environment. In the booklet I call for greater understanding between the communities of business and of non-governmental organizations (NGOs). These are the two constituencies with which I work most closely, and yet my concern is that they do not generally take sufficient time and effort to listen carefully to one another and to search together for positive solutions. This is evidenced by the fact that global economic and environmental summits involving representatives from both constituencies are often marked by division, deadlock and breakdown. The current volume is therefore a contribution to a listening process. Each chapter derives from events in which the Capitalism Project I direct at the London Institute for Contemporary Christianity has played a part, in terms either of organization or of input. While the papers from which they derive were presented with an appropriate level of passion and conviction, each occasion has also been marked by a deepseated regard for divergence of opinion, and an honest and vigorous pursuit of viable ways forward.

Despite this similarity, the contexts represented by the following chapters are many and varied. Three of the chapters – those by David Held, Michael Woolcock and Michael Schluter – are based on papers given at a three-day residential conference on globalization held in the summer of 2002 at Ridley Hall in Cambridge. This conference was organized jointly by the Jubilee Centre, LICC's Capitalism Project and the Ridley Hall Foundation and it involved speakers and delegates from both business and NGOs.

A further four chapters – those by Michael Taylor, Jim Wallis, Ann Pettifor and Timothy Gorringe – derive from presentations given at events in London's financial quarter organized by

JustShare, of which I am Convenor. JustShare is a coalition of mainstream Christian denominations and agencies concerned to address issues of global economic justice in close consultation with senior representatives in both government and international business.

The chapters by Clive Mather and Brian Griffiths began life as presentations given in LICC's 'CEO Series', in which the Capitalism Project plays a leading role. This series, as its title suggests, is aimed specifically at chief executive officers and is generally addressed by senior business leaders.

The chapter by Cynthia Moe-Lobeda is a result of my involvement as the Archbishop of Canterbury's representative on globalization at the consultations of the World Council of Churches, the Lutheran World Federation (LWF), the World Alliance of Reformed Churches and the Roman Catholic and Orthodox Churches. It was at one of these consultations, held in Cartigny (near Geneva) in December 2002, that Cynthia Moe-Lobeda, representing the LWF, presented a paper on which her chapter in this volume in based.

The Epilogue is based on presentations I gave at a seminar entitled 'Consumption, Christianity and Creation' held in July 2002 at Sheffield Hallam University, organized by the university's Centre for Sustainable Consumption, and at a workshop entitled 'Globalization and the Global Environment: The Christian Response?' organized by the John Ray Initiative in London in November 2002.

These chapters represent only a selection from the wealth of papers, lectures and presentations that have been given over the first three years of the Capitalism Project. Many excellent contributions have had to be excluded for reasons of space. While variety of perspective and background has been a key selection criterion, there are inevitable omissions and restrictions. Most of the contributors are from the world of academia, or are closely associated with it; most are either economists or theologians; most are professing Christians; most are male and all are Anglo-Saxon. Nevertheless, each of the contributors is a significant leader in society and all of them are noted for raising a distinct moral voice with regard to the phenomenon of economic globalization. How they understand this phenomenon varies from author to author, and no attempt has been made on my part to furnish them with a working definition. They are in general agreement, however, that contemporary economic globalization involves the increasing integration of national economies into a global market, made possible by the rise of communication and information technology, air travel, large multinational corporations and financial capital. They also appear to agree that, far from being a neutral phenomenon, it has important moral, even religious, dimensions and is shaped not by abstract or invisible economic forces but by the choices and actions of us all.

This volume is divided into three parts. Part I focuses on the contours and potential of globalization. In Chapter 1, David Held maps out the key features of contemporary globalization and the challenges associated with them. He shows how international trade, multinational corporations, transnational production and global financial flows have all grown exponentially. While this does not spell the end of political power, the impact of globalization demands more sophisticated systems of global and regional regulation. A cosmopolitan multilateralism is what is required, and for this European social democratic values and collaborative governance provide a good model.

The two chapters that follow provide, from the perspectives of two Christians involved in multinational business and finance, an assessment both of the potential of economic globalization and of some of its problems. In Chapter 2, Brian Griffiths argues that for globalization to be just it has to be inclusive, serving the needs of the poor. Three policies would help this to be achieved: trade liberalization, the International Finance Facility, and domestic reform in developing countries. Griffiths insists, however, that material prosperity is not the only thing that matters: spiritual enrichment is also important, particularly through the good news of the Christian message and the strengthening of social institutions.

Clive Mather, in Chapter 3, bewails the fact that, in many low-income countries, economic globalization is regarded as an enemy, rather than as an ally. He acknowledges, however, that the activities of global corporations in the developing world give rise to legitimate public concerns: the growing gap between rich and poor, the threat to local diversity, and the exploitation of labour and natural resources. There is a business case, he insists, for allowing such concerns to influence business practice. On the other hand, multinationals are less powerful than is often imagined, and they cannot bear ultimate responsibility for the distribution of wealth or the protection of the environment.

The emphasis in Part II is on critique and alternatives. In Chapter 4, Michael Woolcock draws attention to what he regards as the common ground between theologies and theories of development: an emphasis on the importance of right relationships, rather than on right prices. For him, 'justice' is a necessary though inadequate condition for successful economic development and needs to be supplemented with the biblical theme of 'glory'. There can be little glory, he argues, where there is poverty, which distorts the image of God in humanity and is both symptom and cause of failed social relationships.

Ann Pettifor, in Chapter 5, charts the rapid rise of the financial sector in the global economy. This came about, she argues, as a direct result of deregulation, which was driven by Western governments in order to finance their foreign deficits. Deflationary policies and 'dollarization' have followed, increasing the hardship of many in low-income countries. In the Judaeo-Christian notion of the Sabbath, Pettifor finds support for the introduction of regulation that would place human rights at the centre of economic affairs and would facilitate international insolvency processes for low-income countries that are effectively bankrupt.

Michael Schluter's concern, in Chapter 6, is to engage from a biblical perspective with what he regards as two pillars of contemporary capitalism: the way in which interest operates and limited liability. The former, he argues, minimizes the importance of relationships and community, whereas the latter diminishes the social obligations of company owners (the shareholders). Both 'pillars' have given rise to the giant corporations of today, which represent the concentration of economic power, in contrast to the Bible's insistence on the diffusion of such power, and the separation of ownership from responsibility in contrast to the Bible's insistence that these are held together. In response, Schluter suggests a number of practical changes.

In Chapter 7, Timothy Gorringe finds in the biblical teaching about 'rulers', 'authorities' and 'powers' (Ephesians 6.12) a theological framework for responding to contemporary global economic structures and the spirituality and worldview that undergird them. Globalization, Gorringe argues, is a form of imperialism: it embodies a contemptible account of what it means to be human; it destroys our sense of being at home in the world; and it poses a serious threat to the environment. All spiritual structures are, however, created, fallen, and can be redeemed. From the perspective of redemption, Gorringe concludes, ethics always has to take priority over economics. The 'laws of the market' should be subordinate to the needs of the human and non-human creation.

In Part III the emphasis shifts towards advocating practical change. Cynthia Moe-Lobeda, in Chapter 8, seeks to show how insights from Luther can resource both resistance to neo-liberal globalization and the search for alternatives. She draws these insights from five aspects of his work: his eucharistic ethics, his theology of Christ indwelling creation, his call to certain practices, his belief in the pervasive presence of sin, and his insistence on the presence and power of God in brokenness. She demonstrates how Luther's economic ethics bear striking parallels to those of many of today's critics of economic globalization. His ethics were also deeply subversive, she claims, and he regarded the *communio* (the community of the faithful) as the wellspring of subversive moral agency. In it the incarnate God is embodied as justice-making, self-honouring neighbour-love made manifest in all aspects of life, economics included.

Michael Taylor, in Chapter 9, explains that there are two diametrically opposed views about globalization. For some it is the best hope of the poor; for others it does the poor no good at all. He makes four points about this. First, both sides are united about the unacceptability of poverty, gross inequality and marginalization. Second, there is no moral high ground that can be assumed by either camp, their differences being at least partly technical about how poverty reduction can best be achieved. Third, the choice between the two positions is significantly influenced by where one thinks one's self-interest lies – what divides rich and poor is not self-interest itself but their opportunity to act on it. Fourth, campaigning strategy should not be about the reversal of power between poor and rich but about the sharing of power.

Jim Wallis rounds off this section of the book with a call in Chapter 10 for the strengthening of both faith-based initiatives and the prophetic witness of the Church in the face of global economic inequalities. He argues that the aim of both should be to 'change the wind', rather than to secure incremental changes or to exchange one set of political leaders for another. As faith is the spiritual engine of change, Wallis finds it heartening that old dualisms between the personal and social gospel are breaking down. Fresh initiatives are now under way to restore the integrity of the Bible in our churches, neighbourhoods, workplaces and nations, such as Call to Renewal in the US and JustShare in the UK. They are part of a new faith-based movement for social and economic justice which has hope, rather than anger, at its core.

In the Epilogue, I seek to draw together due recognition of the potential of economic globalization with a critique of some of its impulses and effects. The focus is on the challenge to the environment; the aim is to suggest, in the light of the biblical story of creation, positive ways forward for the global economy that take this challenge seriously. 'Sustainable global capitalism' is offered as an alternative economic model that attaches value to all forms of capital and insists that the use of natural capital needs to be far more productive. Fuel-cell cars, using hydrogen technology, provide an example of how this principle might work in practice. They demonstrate that the interests of the environment and business need not be in conflict with each other. Sustainable global capitalism is therefore global capitalism with a future.

This volume is best understood as providing early engagements with a relatively new issue by people who are not so much detached observers as leading analysts, activists and spokespeople. It is offered in the hope that it will encourage a listening process, contribute to the maturing of a vital debate and stimulate action that will help to realize globalization's potential for good.

Part I

1

Becoming Cosmopolitan: The Dimensions and Challenges of Globalization

DAVID HELD

It is easy to overstate the moment – to overgeneralize from the experience of one event and one time. Thus, for example, we could interpret the events of 11 September 2001 as a, if not the, turning-point in the contemporary period – the moment when the project of globalization met the project of mass terrorism, tinged with global radical Islam. Mass terrorism could be thought of as the challenge to globalization and the spread of such values as the rule of law, democracy and equal liberty. It is a challenge to all these things, of course. But there are other challenges as well, challenges which confront globalization more deeply and broadly. After setting out what I see as the core dimensions of globalization in sections 1 and 2, I will map out some of these challenges in section 3.

There is nothing new about globalization. There have been many phases of globalization over the last two millennia, including the development of world regions, the Age of Discovery, and the spread of empires. But having said this, it is important to note that there is something new about globalization in the current era – that is, about the confluence of change across human activities economic, political, legal, communicative and environmental. We can trace this by measuring the extent, intensity, velocity and impact of human networks and relations in each of the core domains of activity.[1] Given the limitations of space, I will focus here on two of the main driving forces of globalization, the economic and the political.

1. Economic globalization

Today, all countries are engaged in international trade and nearly all trade significant proportions of their national income. If, in the past, trade sometimes formed an enclave largely isolated from the rest of the national economy, it is now integral to the structure of national production in all modern states. The historical evidence shows that international trade has grown to unprecedented levels, both in absolute terms and in relation to national income. Among the states of the OECD (the Organization for Economic Cooperation and Development), trade levels today (measured as a share of GDP) are much greater by comparison with the late nineteenth century (Held *et al.*, 1999: ch. 3). As barriers to trade have fallen across the world, global markets have emerged for many goods and, increasingly, services. World trade (trade in merchandise and services) in 1999 was valued at over $6,800 billion, with exports having grown, as a percentage of world output, from 7.9 per cent in 1913 to 17.2 per cent in 1998 (Maddison, 2001).

After the Second World War, an extensive network of trade emerged which has locked most states – developed and developing – into complex global and regional webs of trade relationships. Although there are major trading blocs in Europe, North America and Asia-Pacific, these are not regional fortresses; on the contrary, they remain open to competition (albeit with systems of incentives and disincentives in place) from the rest of the world. Through the 1980s and 1990s, developing and transition economies became significantly open to trade as well, and their share of world trade, particularly of manufactured goods, rose significantly.

While global exports and trading relations are more important than ever in the world economy and to individual countries for their general prosperity, transnational production is even more significant. To sell to another country, you have increasingly to invest and relocate there. Foreign direct investment reached three times as many countries in 2000 as it did in 1985. The multinational corporation (MNC) has taken economic interconnectedness to new levels. Today, 60,000 MNCs with nearly 820,000 foreign subsidiaries sell $15,680 billion worth of goods and services across the globe each year, and employ twice as many people as they did in 1990. MNCs account for about 25 per cent of world production and 70 per cent of world trade, while their sales are equivalent to almost 50 per cent of world GDP (UNCTAD, 2001; Goldblatt *et al.*, 1997). A quarter to a third of world trade is intra-firm trade between branches of MNCs.

The bulk of the assets of MNCs are typically found in OECD countries and in a relatively small number of developing ones, but their impact is growing everywhere. Of total world foreign direct investment in 2000, 95 per cent went to 30 countries. Over the last few decades, however, developing economies' share of foreign investment flows (inwards and outwards) and of world exports has increased considerably (UNCTAD, 2001; 1998; Castells, 1996). The newly industrialized countries of East Asia and Latin America have become an increasingly important destination for OECD investment and an increasingly significant source of OECD imports – São Paulo, it is sometimes said, is Germany's largest industrial city (Dicken, 1998). By the late 1990s almost 50 per cent of total world manufacturing jobs were located in developing economies, while over 60 per cent of developing-country exports to the industrialized world were manufactured goods, a twelvefold increase in less than four decades (UNDP, 1998). Contemporary economic globalization, albeit highly unevenly spread, is not just an OECD phenomenon but embraces all continents and regions.

Alongside transnational production networks, the power of global finance has become central to economic globalization. World financial flows have grown exponentially, especially since the 1970s. Daily turnover on the foreign exchange markets exceeds $1.2 trillion, and billions of dollars of financial assets are traded globally, particularly through derivative products (BIS, 2001). Few countries today are insulated from the dynamics of global financial markets, although their relationship to these markets differs markedly between North and South. International banking, bond issues and equities trading have risen from negligible to historically significant levels. The level of cross-border transactions is unprecedented. Where once international financial markets operated to fund wars, trade and long-term investment, much of their activity is now speculative, and this is a significant change. However, to say that it is speculative is not to say that it is tantamount to gambling in all respects. Many financial institutions and MNCs are drawn into the foreign exchange markets in order to hedge against changes in currency valuations so as to protect their long-term trading positions (cf. Strange, 1996).

The 1997 East Asian crisis forcibly illustrated the impact of global financial markets. The financial disruption triggered by the collapse of the Thai baht demonstrated new levels of economic connectedness. The Asian 'tiger' economies had benefited from the rapid increase of financial flows to developing countries in the 1990s and were widely held as positive examples to the rest of the world. But the heavy flows of short-term capital, often channelled into speculative activity, could be quickly reversed, causing currencies to fall dramatically and far in excess of any real economic imbalances. The inability of the existing international financial regime (the International Monetary Fund (IMF), the Bank for International Settlements, etc.) to manage the turmoil created a wide-ranging debate on its future institutional architecture.

It is easy to misrepresent the political significance of the globalization of economic activity. National and international economic management remain feasible (Held *et al.*, 1999; Hirst and Thompson, 1999). Many states continue to be immensely powerful, and enjoy access to a formidable range of resources, infrastructural capacity and technologies of coordination and control. The continuing lobbying by MNCs of states and inter-governmental organizations (IGOs) (the World Trade Organization (WTO), for example) confirms the enduring importance of states to the mediation and regulation of global economic activity. Yet economic globalization has significant and discernible impacts which alter the balance of resources, economic and political, within and across borders, requiring more sophisticated, developed systems of global and regional regulation (see section 3 below).

2. Political globalization

Economic globalization has not occurred in an empty political space; there has been a shift in the nature and form of political organization as well. The distinctive form this has taken in the contemporary period is the emergence of 'global politics' – the increasingly extensive form of political activity. Political decisions and actions in one part of the world can rapidly develop worldwide ramifications. Sites of political action and/or decision-making can become linked through rapid communications into complex networks of political interaction. Associated with this 'stretching' of politics is a frequent intensification of global processes such that 'action at a distance' permeates the social conditions and cognitive worlds of specific places or policy communities (Giddens, 1990: ch. 2). As a consequence, developments at the global level – whether economic, social or environmental – can acquire almost instantaneous local consequences and vice versa.

The idea of global politics challenges the traditional distinctions between the domestic/international, territorial/non-territorial, inside/outside, as embedded in modern conceptions of 'the political' (Held *et al.*, 1999: chs 1, 2 and 8). It also highlights the richness and complexity of the interconnections that transcend states and societies in the global order. Global politics today, moreover, is anchored not just in traditional geopolitical concerns but also in a large diversity of economic, social and ecological questions. Pollution, drugs, money-laundering, human rights and terrorism are among an increasing number of transnational policy issues which cut across territorial jurisdictions and existing political alignments, and which require international cooperation for their effective resolution.

Nations, peoples and organizations are linked, in addition, by many new forms of communication that range across borders. The revolution in communication and information technology has established virtually instantaneous worldwide links which, when combined with jet transportation, have dramatically altered the nature of political communication. The intimate connection between 'physical setting', 'social situation' and politics which distinguished most political associations from pre-modern to modern times has been ruptured; the new communication systems create new experiences, new modes of understanding and new frames of political reference independently of direct contact with particular peoples, issues or events. The speed with which the events of 9/11 reverberated around the world and made mass terrorism a global issue is one poignant example.

In mapping political globalization, it is important to explore the way in which the sovereign state now lies at the intersection of a vast array of international regimes and organizations that have been established to manage whole areas of transnational activity (trade, financial flows, crime, etc.) and collective policy problems. The rapid growth of transnational issues and problems has involved a spread of layers of governance both within and across political boundaries. It has been marked by the transformation of aspects of territorially based political decision-making, the development of regional and global organizations and institutions, and the emergence of regional and global law.

This can be illustrated by a number of developments including, most obviously, the rapid emergence of multilateral agencies and organizations. New forms of multilateral and global politics have been established involving governments, IGOs and a wide variety of transnational pressure groups and international non-governmental organizations (INGOs). At the beginning of the twentieth century there were just 37 IGOs and 176 INGOs, while in 1996 there were 1,830 IGOs and 38,243 INGOs (Union of International Associations, 1997). In addition, there has been a very substantial development in the number of international treaties in force, as well as in the number of international regimes, all of which alters the situational context of states (Held *et al.*, 1999: chs 1–2).

To this pattern of extensive political interconnectedness can be added the dense web of activity of the key international policy-making fora, including the UN, G7, IMF, WTO and EU. In the middle of the nineteenth century, two or three interstate conferences or congresses took place each year; today the number totals over 4,000. National governments are increasingly locked into an array of global, regional and multi-layered systems of governance – and they can barely monitor it all, let alone stay in command. Foreign and domestic policies have become chronically intermeshed, making the national coordination and control of government policy increasingly problematic.

Interlaced with these political and legal transformations are changes in the world military order. Few states, except perhaps for the US and China, can now realistically contemplate unilateralism or neutrality as a credible defence strategy. Global and regional security institutions have become more salient as a collectivization of national security has evolved (Clark, 2001). But it is not just the institutions of defence that have become multinational. In the production of military hardware, the age of 'national champions' has been superseded by one in which few countries are wholly autonomous, not least because of an increased reliance on electronics, which are themselves the products of highly globalized industries (Held *et al.*, 1999: ch. 2).

The paradox and novelty of the globalization of organized violence is that national security today is increasingly a collective or multilateral affair. For the first time in history, the one thing that did most to give modern nation-states a focus and a purpose, and which has always been at the very heart of modern statehood, can now be realized effectively only if nation-states come together and pool resources, intelligence and authority.

Political communities can no longer be thought of (if they ever could be with any validity) as discrete worlds or as self-enclosed political spaces; they are enmeshed in complex structures of overlapping forces, relations and networks. Clearly, these are structured by inequality and hierarchy. However, even the most powerful among them do not remain unaffected by the changing conditions and processes of regional and global entrenchment. How should we understand these? And how should we understand their key implications and consequences?

3. The challenges of globalization

Contemporary globalization has elements in common with past phases, but is distinguished by unique organizational features,

David Held

creating a world in which the extensive reach of human relations and networks is matched by their relative high-intensity, high-velocity and high-impact propensity across many facets of social life. The result is the emergence of a global economy, 24-hour trading in financial markets, new forms of international law, and the development of regional and global governance structures. To this has been added the creation of new global systemic problems, including global warming, Aids, mass terrorism, market volatility, the international drugs trade and under-regulated genetic engineering. All this poses a number of striking challenges.

First, contemporary processes of globalization and regionalization create overlapping networks of power which cut across territorial boundaries; as such they put pressure on, and strain, a world order designed in accordance with the principle of exclusive sovereign rule over a bounded territory. Effective political power is now shared and bartered by diverse forces and agencies, public and private, at national, regional and international levels. Moreover, the idea of a self-determining people or political community can no longer be located within the boundaries of a single nation-state alone. Some of the most fundamental forces and processes that determine the nature of life-chances are now beyond the reach of individual nation-states.

In the past, nation-states principally resolved their differences over boundary matters by pursuing *raison d'état* backed by diplomatic initiatives and, ultimately, by coercive means. But this power logic is singularly inadequate to resolve the many complex issues – from economic regulation, resource depletion and environmental degradation to mass terrorism – which engender, at seemingly ever greater speeds, an intermeshing of 'national fortunes'. We are, as Kant most eloquently put it, 'unavoidably side by side'. In a world where powerful states make decisions not just for their peoples but for others as well, and where transnational forces cut across the boundaries of national communities in diverse ways, the questions of who should be accountable to whom, and on what basis, do not easily resolve themselves.

Second, existing political institutions, national and international, are weakened by three crucial regulatory and political gaps (Kaul *et al.*, 1999: xixff.):

a *jurisdictional* gap – the discrepancy between a regionalized and globalized world and national units of policy-making, giving rise to the problem of externalities and who is responsible for them;

a *participation* gap – the failure of the existing international system to give adequate voice to many leading global actors, state and non-state; and

an *incentive* gap – the challenges posed by the fact that, in the absence of any supranational entity to regulate the supply and use of global public goods, many states will seek to free ride and/or fail to find durable collective solutions to pressing transnational problems.

Third, these political disjunctures are conjoined by an additional gap – what might be called a 'moral gap'; that is, a gap defined by:

(a) the fact that over 1.2 billion people live on less than $1 a day; 46 per cent of the world's population live on less than $2 a day; and 20 per cent of the world's population enjoy 80 per cent of its income;
(b) commitments and values of, at best, 'passive indifference' to this, marked by UN expenditure per annum of $1.25 billion (plus the cost of peace-keeping); US per annum confectionery expenditure of $27 billion; US per annum alcohol expenditure of $70 billion; and US per annum expenditure on cars that is through the roof (over $550 billion).

This is not an anti-America statement, of course. Equivalent EU figures could have been highlighted.

Seemingly obvious questions arise. Would anyone freely choose such a state of affairs? Would anyone freely choose a distributional pattern of scarce goods and services which causes hundreds of millions of people to suffer serious harm and disadvantage independent of their will and consent (and 50,000 dying every day of malnutrition and poverty-related causes),

unless they had a privileged stake in the existing social hierarchy? Would anyone freely endorse a situation in which the
annual cost of supplying basic education to all children is $6
billion, water and sanitation $9 billion, and basic health to all
$13 billion, while annually $8 billion is spent in the US on
cosmetics, nearly $20 billion on jewellery and $17 billion (in the
US and Europe) on pet food?[2] Before an impartial court of
moral reason, it is hard to see how an affirmative answer to
these questions could be defended. That global inequalities
spark conflict and contestation can hardly be a surprise, especially given the visibility of the world's lifestyles in an age of
mass media.

Fourth, there has been a shift from relatively discrete national
communication and economic systems to their more complex
and diverse enmeshment at regional and global levels, and from
national government to multilevel governance. Yet there are few
grounds for thinking that a parallel 'globalization' of political
identities has taken place. One exception to this is to be found
among the elites of the global order – the networks of experts
and specialists, senior administrative personnel and transnational business executives – and those who track and contest
their activities, the loose constellation of social movements
(including the 'anti-globalization' movement), trade-unionists
and (a few) politicians and intellectuals. But these groups are
not typical. Thus, we live with a challenging paradox – that
governance is becoming increasingly a multilevel, intricately
institutionalized and spatially dispersed activity, while represent-
ation, loyalty and identity remain stubbornly rooted in traditional ethnic, regional and national communities (cf. Wallace,
1999).

Hence, the shift from government to multilayered governance, from national economies to economic globalization, is a
potentially unstable shift, capable of reversal in some respects
and certainly capable of engendering a fierce reaction – a reaction drawing on nostalgia, romanticized conceptions of political
community, hostility to outsiders (refugees) and a search for a
pure national state (for example in the politics of Haider in
Austria, Le Pen in France, and so on). But this reaction itself is
likely to be highly unstable, and perhaps a relatively short- or

medium-term phenomenon. To understand why this is so, nationalism has to be disaggregated.

As 'cultural nationalism' it is, and in all likelihood will remain, central to people's identity; however, as 'political nationalism' – the assertion of the exclusive political priority of national identity and the national interest – it cannot deliver many sought-after public goods without seeking accommodation with others, in and through regional and global collaboration. In this respect, only an international or, better still, cosmopolitan outlook can ultimately accommodate itself to the political challenges of a more global era, marked by overlapping communities of fate and multilevel/multilayered politics. Unlike political nationalism, cosmopolitanism registers and reflects the multiplicity of issues, questions, processes and problems that affect and bind people together irrespective of where they were born or reside.

We require a shift from a club-driven and executive-led multilateralism – which is typically secretive and exclusionary – to a more transparent, accountable and just form of governance – a socially backed, cosmopolitan multilateralism. The core requirements of this are:

(a) recognition of the increasing interconnectedness of political communities in diverse domains (including the social, the economic and the environmental);
(b) the development of an understanding of overlapping 'collective fortunes' which require collective norms and solutions – locally, nationally, regionally and globally;
(c) the acknowledgement of the need for more decisions and more effective and accountable decisions at transnational levels;
(d) the extension and transformation of our existing multilevel, multilayered polity, running from the local to the regional and global, so that it adopts, within its *modus operandi*, the principles of transparency, accountability and democracy.

Cosmopolitan multilateralization cannot be built on the American model of geopolitics and international engagement, especially as conceived by the Republican right after 9/11, which constitutes a new form of global unilateralism. The European Union, based on social democratic values and collaborative governance, points a way forward. Yet within the EU there is a serious danger of a deep split developing between elite and mass politics, and the alienation of the popular will.

Like nationalism, cosmopolitanism is a cultural and political project, but with one difference: it is better adapted and suited to our regional and global age. But the arguments in support of this have yet to be won in the public sphere; and we lose them at our peril.

It is important to return to 9/11 and to say what it means in this context. One cannot accept the burden of putting justice right in one realm of life – physical security and political co-operation among defence establishments – without at the same time seeking to put it right elsewhere. If the political and the security, the social and the economic dimensions of justice are separated in the long term – as is the tendency in the global order today – the prospects of a peaceful and civil society will be bleak indeed. Popular support against terrorism, as well as against political violence and exclusionary politics of all kinds, depends upon convincing people that there is a legal, responsive and specific way of addressing their grievances. Without this sense of confidence in public institutions the defeat of terrorism and intolerance becomes a hugely difficult task, if it can be achieved at all. Globalization without cosmopolitanism could fail.

Notes

1. I have tried to do this with Anthony McGrew in *Global Transformations* (1999) and in *Globalization/Anti-globalization* (2002).
2. These figures are drawn from the US economic census for 1997 and from www.wwflearning.co.uk/news/features_0000000354.asp.

References

Bank for International Settlements (BIS) (2001), *BIS Quarterly Review December*. Geneva.

Castells, M. (1996), *The Rise of Network Society*. Blackwell, Oxford.

Clark, I. (2001), *The Post-Cold War Order: The Spoils of Peace*. Oxford University Press, Oxford.

Dicken, P. (1998), *Global Shift*. Paul Chapman, London.

Giddens, A. (1990), *The Consequences of Modernity*. Polity Press, Cambridge.

Goldblatt, D., Held, D., McGrew, A. and Perraton, J. (1997), 'Economic Globalization and the Nation-State: Shifting Balances of Power', *Alternatives* 22(3): 269–85.

Held, D. and McGrew, A. (2002), *Globalization/Anti-globalization*. Polity Press, Cambridge.

Hirst, P. and Thompson, G. (1999), *Globalization in Question*, 2nd edn. Polity Press, Cambridge.

Kaul, I., Grunberg, I. and Stern, M. (1999), *Global Public Goods: International Cooperation in the Twenty-First Century*. Oxford University Press, Oxford.

Maddison, A. (2001), *The World Economy: A Millennial Perspective*. OECD Development Studies Centre, Paris.

Strange, S. (1996), *The Retreat of the State*. Cambridge University Press, Cambridge.

UNCTAD (1998), *The Least Developed Countries 1998*. UN Conference on Trade and Development, Geneva.

UNCTAD (2001), *World Investment Report 2001*. UN Conference on Trade and Development, Geneva.

UNDP (1998), *Globalization and Liberalization*. Oxford University Press, New York.

Union of International Associations (1997), *Yearbook of International Organizations 1996–7*. K. G. Saur, Munich.

Wallace, W. (1999), 'The Sharing of Sovereignty: The European Paradox?', *Political Studies* 47(3), special issue.

2

The Role of Trade, Aid and Domestic Reform in the Fight against Global Poverty

BRIAN GRIFFITHS

Globalization has created enormous opportunities to reduce world poverty. During the 1980s and 1990s, many developing countries were able to break into global markets, raise their standard of living and reduce poverty. The most dramatic example was China, followed by India, but success stories may also be found in other countries in Asia and Latin America. However, one of the most disconcerting facts of globalization is its uneven impact. Globalization is no panacea for poverty. Over these same years other developing countries have suffered declining incomes and rising poverty. The present situation in sub-Saharan Africa is especially dire as its population accounts for around 95 per cent of those living on less than $1 a day. GDP per capita in the region declined in the 1990s by just over half a percentage point each year. Twenty countries, which count for more than half of the region's population, are poorer now than they were in 1990. According to the UN, the number of undernourished people in the region has reached 200 million, with malnutrition being the leading cause of death for children under five.

In over one-third of African countries, every other child is out of school. On present trends, universal primary school education will not be provided in Africa until 2100. Some 25 million people in sub-Saharan Africa are HIV positive; 10 million children have been orphaned by Aids. Life expectancy in 13 countries has fallen below 45 years. All of this confirms the judgement Kofi Annan gave in his acceptance speech for the

Nobel Peace Prize, that 'the main losers in today's very unequal world are not those who are too exposed to globalization, but those who have been left out'.

The causes of this situation are complex. The prices of exports from sub-Saharan countries have declined. Protection has excluded African goods from the markets of the European Union and North America. Weak domestic governance, misdirected policies, corruption, and an investment climate unconducive to growth have all played a part. Most recently, the spread of HIV/Aids and other diseases, droughts, famines and wars has only compounded the problem.

At the UN Millennium Summit of 2000, more than 140 world leaders signed up to support a major campaign to reduce world poverty. Progress, however, has been slow. The danger of this is that people become resigned to a seemingly hopeless situation. Official aid is by and large perceived as having been wasted, squandered or stolen. The leadership of Mobutu, Amin and Bokassa proved to be a disaster. In South Africa, crime and violence are at unacceptably high levels. The pandemic of HIV/Aids is a tax on business and undermines the two attractions of foreign investment, cheap labour and rapidly growing markets. Until the countries of sub-Saharan Africa set their own houses in order, so the argument goes, then short of basic relief there is little the rest of the world can do to help.

For the Christian, such an attitude of resignation is simply not an option. In this chapter I wish to look at the persistence of poverty in a world of globalization, but from a Christian perspective. After examining poverty within a Christian framework, I will discuss several policies to combat poverty, specifically in the areas of trade, aid and necessary reforms in developing countries.

The God of the poor

One of the unmistakable facts of both the Old Testament and the New is that the God of the Bible is the God of the poor. Throughout the Old Testament, Jews were obliged to care for the poor, typically the widow, the orphan and the stranger. The requirement in the Torah to make special provision for the poor was not a matter of charity, generosity or pity but of justice. The responsibility to care for those in need was not a matter of choice; it was an obligation required by God. The laws relating to land, labour and capital were designed to ensure that no-one was permanently excluded from having a stake in economic life. The reason for the special concern for the poor was that poverty defaced the image of God in his creation. Poverty is demeaning, unjust and a waste of human potential.

The same theme is continued in the New Testament. In his first public statement, Jesus outlined his mission by quoting from the prophecy of Isaiah: 'The Spirit of the Lord is on me, because he has anointed me to preach good news to the poor' (Luke 4.18).

His audience was Jewish. They would have understood his reference to Isaiah in the context of the whole of Old Testament teaching. While Jesus extended his teaching to include spiritual need, the fact remains that those who were poor in material terms held a unique place in his ministry.

In the parable of the Last Judgement, so vividly described in St Matthew's Gospel, Jesus made it very clear that we will be judged personally by how we respond to the hungry, the thirsty, the stranger, the sick, the impoverished and those in prison (Matthew 25.31–46). It is because of this that for the last 2,000 years the Christian Church has felt a special calling to work among the deprived, the excluded and the disadvantaged, in slums and shanty towns, in inner cities and rapidly growing cities, by providing schools and hospitals, orphanages and hospices, shelter and rescue programmes.

The Roman Catholic Church has expressed its commitment as 'a preferential option for the poor'. In his 1991 encyclical *Centesimus Annus*, Pope John Paul II addressed the issue of poverty in developing countries. He called for a special effort to mobilize resources for the purpose of economic growth and development, arguing:

> The poor ask for the right to share in enjoying material goods and to make good use of their capacity for work, thus creating a world that is more just and prosperous for all. The advancement of the poor constitutes a great opportunity for

the moral, cultural and even economic growth of all humanity.[1]

There are five aspects of Christian teaching regarding the poor that need emphasis.

First, because each person is sacred in the eyes of God, every human life possesses infinite dignity and worth. Individuals who are undernourished, without clean water, suffering from disease and lacking basic education cannot realize their potential as human beings. They cannot participate fully in economic life. Poverty is a scar on God's creation, and so it must be tackled. For globalization to be just it must be inclusive.

Second, Christians have an obligation to respond to the needs of the poor. It is not a matter of personal choice or preference. The teaching of Jesus is a challenge to individuals, to communities, to churches and to our society as a whole. At a personal level it is a challenge based on compassion, and at a political level it is a challenge based on justice. It is above all a challenge for each individual Christian, family and community to be involved directly by giving time and money.

Third, in both the Old and the New Testaments the poor are not some class or socio-economic group, but individuals, each with a story to tell. The mandate to help the poor is a mandate to help individual persons trapped in poverty. In the Old Testament it is a concern for the widow, the orphan and the stranger, in the New Testament for the hungry, the homeless, the sick, the outcast and those in prison. By contrast, official development aid is a transfer of taxpayers' money in rich countries to the finance ministries of governments in poor countries. It is impersonal and only indirectly concerned with poor people themselves. This is not an argument against official transfers of wealth from rich to developing countries, simply that its delivery and effectiveness must be measured in personal terms, not general statistics.

Fourth, tackling poverty by raising the material standard of living is important, but only part of the challenge. A concept of development that is restricted to economics is deficient. Development must also be concerned with the communities in which people live. Strengthening family life is important, because family life that is based on Judaeo-Christian teaching will be conducive to eradicating poverty. Schools that have a Christian ethos will balance material prosperity with public service. Hospitals founded from a Christian concern will treat the patients holistically, not just medically. In these and other areas, Christian charities have a critical role to play in developing robust and caring communities in the process of removing poverty.

Finally, a Christian response must be concerned with the whole of a person's life. This includes the economic, the social and the political, but it must also include the spiritual. The temptation to turn stones into bread was rejected by Jesus with the words 'man does not live by bread alone'. In the context of our responsibilities to developing countries, Pope John Paul II stated it very clearly:

> The apex of development is the exercise of the right and duty to seek God, to know him and to live in accordance with that knowledge . . . The exercise and development of this right includes the right to discover and freely to accept Jesus Christ, who is man's true good.[2]

A Marshall Plan for Africa

As we have already seen, the one area of the world that globalization has bypassed is Africa. Although the situation in Africa is desperately serious, there are signs of hope. Uganda, Mozambique and Angola have managed to buck the trends in the region. In these countries poverty is declining. Although not attracting sufficient foreign investment, the South African economy is growing at roughly 3 per cent a year. For the trends in sub-Saharan Africa as a whole to be reversed, however, a new, imaginative and comprehensive initiative will be required. We need, as some have suggested, an African equivalent of the Marshall Plan of the 1940s.

At present there are three separate initiatives that could have an impact in reducing global poverty. One is the Doha round of trade liberalization being conducted by the World Trade Organization (WTO), the second is the International Finance

Facility proposed by Gordon Brown, the UK Chancellor of the Exchequer, and the third is the setting up of the New Partnership for Africa's Development (NEPAD). Although the Marshall Plan was concerned with reconstruction, not development, these initiatives taken together could be a major boost to stimulating the private sector in sub-Saharan Africa, preparing the way for foreign investment, creating jobs and reducing poverty. Not only that, but each of them is firmly rooted in a Judaeo-Christian framework.

Trade liberalization

One of the ironies of world poverty is that although globalization has bypassed the economies of sub-Saharan Africa, these countries have in fact been heavily involved in trade. The region exports 30 per cent of its GDP. One reason why trade has had such little impact is that many of its exports have been primary commodities, the prices of which have kept falling. At the same time Africa has found it extremely difficult to export agricultural products and low-grade textiles, as well as to diversify into high value-added products because of the protection they have faced, especially in the United States and the European Union.

Import tariffs on industrial products were high in sub-Saharan Africa in the mid-twentieth century. Today they are less than 4 per cent. Meanwhile, EU agricultural tariffs stand at over 17 per cent and those of the US at 11 per cent. In the round of trade negotiations that took place in Doha in November 2001, Professor Joseph Stiglitz, who was then Chief Economist of the World Bank, estimated that sub-Saharan Africa would actually be worse off as a result of the trade round. The reason was that while African countries were forced to open up their markets to imports, the markets in which their exports had a competitive advantage (low-grade textiles and agricultural goods) were not opened up to foreign competition. Official development aid has been roughly $50 billion a year, while subsidies in rich countries to their own farmers have totalled $350 billion a year. While farmers benefit, the absurdity of the policy is that taxpayers pay more and consumers face higher food prices.

It is because of these distortions that the current protection of agriculture by rich countries has come in for such stinging criticism: 'wholly objectionable and unjustifiable' (House of Lords Select Committee Report); 'has marginalised the ability of many developing countries to participate fully in the global economy and to access many of the benefits of globalisation' (Australian Department of Foreign Affairs and Trade); 'a colossal and very serious problem' (Nicholas Stern, World Bank); 'the European Union's agricultural policy does positive harm to African agriculture. I have been quoted as calling it a "crime against humanity" and I stand by that' (Lord Desai, London School of Economics[3]). If the constant cry of the Old Testament prophets against injustice has any application in today's world, it is surely to the issue of agriculture.

Many detailed examples could be given to support these views. Ghana attempted to develop its tomato industry with tomato canning factories, only to discover that the Italians dumped surplus tomatoes in Ghana to kill off the trade. Mozambique produces 200,000 tonnes of sugar per year at half the cost of European sugar beet. Quotas meant that in 2001 it could only sell 8,000 tonnes to the EU and 12,000 to the US. Meanwhile, European consumers and taxpayers subsidize sugar beet production to the tune of $2.4 billion per year, while Mozambique, with slightly higher quotas in 2004, will be deprived of the opportunity to earn $150 billion in export earnings. Throughout the twentieth century there were many noteworthy and distinguished voices which argued that free trade was not in the interests of the developing countries. However, the experience of the so-called 'Asian tigers' (Hong Kong, Malaysia, Taiwan and Singapore), which broke the mould and experienced rapid growth, followed later by Thailand, Brazil and Mexico, undermined the intellectual case that had been put forward to support protectionism. A recent study by the World Bank contrasted the fortunes of two groups of countries during the 1990s as they related to trade. One group, including China, Mexico and India, doubled its exports as a percentage of GDP over this period. In these countries GDP per capita growth was 5 per cent per year. In the other group, which included Russia and countries in

Africa and the Middle East, the share of exports relative to GDP fell. In these countries GDP per capita growth averaged just 1 per cent per year.

Trade is important, yet it is not the only cause of economic growth. Growth depends on many internal factors, such as the skills of the labour force, the robustness of property rights, the infrastructure for transportation and communications, the rewards for risk-taking, monetary and fiscal stability, expertise in accounts, management and law, transparency and integrity in public administration. In a long list of possible causes of growth, foreign trade would not be number one. But if the other factors are beginning to be put in place, then openness to trade and investment can be a powerful stimulus to development. Hence the critical need for the EU and the US to reduce trade barriers and open up new possibilities for developing countries, and hence the importance of the current Doha round of trade negotiations, which is geared to helping developing countries.

The International Finance Facility

The other area in which rich countries can take the initiative is official development aid (ODA). Throughout the 1990s, aid as a percentage of the GDP of rich countries fell to just over 0.2 per cent. The Pearson Report on development (1964) set the benchmark for subsequent discussion on this subject by making the target 0.7 per cent for rich countries. The level of present contributions looks set to increase. At a meeting of G7 Finance Ministers in February 2003, Gordon Brown proposed doubling development aid from $50 billion to $100 billion a year up to 2015, the year world leaders have earmarked for reaching certain development goals.

The centrepiece of Gordon Brown's proposals is the setting up of an International Finance Facility (IFF). On the basis of donor countries making long-term (over a period of, say, 15 years) rather than annual commitments, the aim is to raise, based on those commitments, an extra $50 billion per year between now and 2015 from the capital markets. These funds will be raised by a new body, the IFF, and then handed back to countries in proportion to their long-term commitments so that they can be dispersed on a bilateral basis as ODA.

At first sight, a proposal that focuses on aid has a tired, 1960s ring to it. Government-to-government aid has been prone to misuse in subsidizing incompetence, corruption and bad policies. Even the World Bank has admitted that aid to countries such as Zaire and Zambia has been little short of an unmitigated disaster. All too often the success of aid has been judged by dollars spent, not by poverty reduced. However, the fact that some aid has been wasted, squandered or stolen is not an argument against all aid. Moreover, Brown's case for increased aid is critically different from that made in the past.

In the first place, this time the effectiveness of aid will be judged by measurable outputs, not monetary inputs: by the miles of roads built, the numbers of vaccinations carried out, the performance of children at schools and the amount of clean water provided. These can be validated by independent auditors.

Second, Brown is explicit that the engine driving growth in all countries is the private sector. Without a thriving private sector, African countries will never defeat poverty. For a private sector to develop, developing country governments must provide well-defined rights to property, their enforcement in law and reduced red tape and regulation. If the private sector is to prosper, it needs reduced trade barriers (by committing to the Doha agenda), and improved incentives for risk-taking. Without clean water, universal primary schooling, more roads and better public health, the growth of the market economy will be restricted.

Third, a critical element of these proposals is conditionality. Funds will only be dispersed to countries that are committed to a stable framework of prices and public spending and support of the market economy. This means greater transparency in the conduct of monetary and fiscal policy, timely publication of relevant data, openness to regular assessment by the International Monetary Fund, more open public administration and the rooting out of corruption. Likely candidates to receive extra funding at present in sub-Saharan Africa would be Tanzania, Uganda and Mozambique. If countries do not implement sound policies, continued funding would be wasted, even counterproductive, and would therefore come to an end. Increased aid to the poorest countries is a moral imperative – but so is its effective disbursement.

Although the Brown proposal is about jointly raising more funds from the international capital markets, a key feature is that each donor country will retain the right to disperse the extra funds to those countries that are committed to meeting its conditions. This proposal is not about raising funds, handing them over to the World Bank and then letting the World Bank decide on how the funds should be dispersed. Taxpayers will have control of how these funds are spent because donor countries, not development banks, will be in the driving seat.

Again, unlike present aid, the bulk of this funding will be through grants, not loans. Too often in the past, development banks fostered a lending culture in which success was judged by the growth in the volume of lending, not of poverty reduction. Taxpayers in donor countries are far more likely to support foreign aid if it is in grant form, if it is transparent, and if its effectiveness is monitored.

Lastly, these proposals can be used to promote more effective delivery. Not all aid need go to governments. Private sector providers, including non-governmental organizations (NGOs) and charities, could be awarded contracts on a competitive basis. It might even be made a condition. Failure to deliver on earlier projects would be a handicap in future bids. External auditors would scrutinize the use of funds and measure increased outputs. The donor countries might withhold final payment until the auditors had signed off. In sub-Saharan Africa, peer review by the African countries of NEPAD is an important step forward to Africa owning its own development. But for peer reviews to work, they must embody international practice and be completely transparent.

It might be argued that if the private sector of a developing country is already taking off, then foreign aid is unnecessary. However, even if dynamic, private sector-led economies emerge in the world's poorest countries in the foreseeable future, they will not of themselves produce clean water, new roads or more teachers, nor will they solve the problem of public health in the next decade or two. While the market may generate sufficient wealth to take care of these problems in the long run (that favourite expression of economists), the sheer magnitude of the problem demands action now. Sustained private sector growth is dependent on an effective public infrastructure.

Gordon Brown's proposals mark a watershed in tackling world poverty. Doubling aid, changing the terms on which it is given, strengthening the private sector and speeding up reform in poor countries is the only effective way to respond to the current crisis. This is not a party-political issue. It deserves the support of all businesses, NGOs and political parties in rich countries.

The New Partnership for Africa's Development (NEPAD)

The rich countries can and should take certain initiatives. But trade and aid will never be a substitute for African countries committing themselves to developing their own market economies within the context of strong and fair legal systems and transparent public administration. This emphasis on the potential benefits from the private sector is crucial. Throughout most of the 1990s, lending and investment by the world's development banks represented only 2 per cent of total private sector capital flow to developing countries. The success of the 'Asian tigers' in the 1960s, then Mexico, Brazil, Thailand and Malaysia, and China in the 1990s, was critically dependent on all these countries attracting foreign investment, which in turn reflected investor confidence in their reform policies.

In establishing NEPAD in October 2001, African countries took an important step forward. NEPAD is a declaration that Africa's development is Africa's responsibility, and that Africa's development plan should be African-led and African-owned. Its long-term objectives are to eradicate poverty in Africa and put African countries on a path of sustainable growth and development so that Africa will no longer be marginalized in the globalization process. It is a comprehensive proposal, ranging from strengthening mechanisms for conflict prevention to greater transparency and accountability in government, monetary and fiscal stability, enforcing the legal framework, revitalizing education and health and setting out development initiatives in agriculture, trade, transport, water, manufacturing and mining. It recognizes that the private sector will be the engine of growth, with governments concentrating on the development of infrastructure and the creation of stable macro-environments.

Its implementation will depend critically on an African peer review mechanism. The concept of a peer review mechanism is not new, and works well for the UK in the OECD (the Organization for Economic Cooperation and Development). It remains to be seen how it will work in practice in NEPAD. The failure to act over Zimbabwe's land reforms does not augur well. It would be extraordinary if NEPAD were to achieve its objectives, or anything approaching them, in most African countries, but its value lies in the fact that it provides a framework which any African country can use as a basis for internal reforms in the interests of economic growth.

Conclusion

The developments outlined above offer hope for a major attack on world poverty. African countries have taken a major step forward in setting up NEPAD. Members of the WTO have signed up to phase out protection for agriculture and products of low-technology industries. The International Finance Facility holds the prospect of doubling the flow of aid from rich countries to poor ones.

Each of these proposals makes sense on its own. Taken together, they could be a formidable attack on global poverty. They cannot be labelled as either left or right. They recognize the importance of the private sector and of trade and investment flows, but they are also concerned with equity and justice. Because of that they deserve the support of political parties across the spectrum, of NGOs and of business. They are the greatest opportunity we have had for more than a decade to remedy the scandalous state of world poverty.

To leave it there, however, would be to obscure and neglect the spiritual dimension. Economic development raises many issues, such as the ethos of companies operating in poor countries, the fairness of land reform, the removal of protective barriers to trade, integrity in the interface between government and the private sector, and regard for stakeholders. For the Christian, these cannot be addressed without regard to the framework of private property rights and justice that is central to the whole of the Bible. Tackling poverty through Christian-based initiatives will also mean that the good news of the Christian message, which offers hope to everyone regardless of material circumstance, will be at the heart of the reform process.

Notes

1. Pope John Paul II, *Centesimus Annus* (1991), Section 28.
2. Pope John Paul II, *Centesimus Annus*, Section 29.
3. Select Committee on Economic Affairs, *Globalization*, First Report, Session 2002–03 (House of Lords, London, November 2002).

3

Combining Principle with Profit:
A Business Response to the Challenges
of Globalization

CLIVE MATHER

Globalization is a concept which society is struggling to accept. Perhaps due to a lack of understanding about whether it will help or hinder future generations, people seem to have not yet made up their minds about whether globalization is a force for good or for bad.

I am writing not only from my perspective as Chairman of Shell UK, but also as a parent, a Christian and a member of the global community. These roles are all closely intertwined: even if I wanted to write solely as a business leader, it would be impossible. The simple truth is that the values I attempt to live up to in my personal life – honesty, trust, respect – are equally valid in business life. My views on globalization, therefore, do not arise out of my business life alone.

Throughout my working life I have had to grapple with complex ethical and social issues. I was a Director of Shell South Africa during some of the darkest years of the apartheid regime. There were many at that time urging Shell, along with other UK companies, to leave South Africa. The Shell view was that staying in South Africa, and providing a positive model of what business could be like, offered hope for a future without apartheid. It is now clear that Shell took the right course of action. More importantly, Nelson Mandela and others in the anti-apartheid movement have since stated that they continue to see Shell as an important partner in the rebuilding of their country.

In too many of the poorest parts of the world, globalization is seen as the enemy of 'partnership' and 'rebuilding', rather than as its ally. As spelt out by the UN Secretary-General, Kofi Annan, the true picture is rather more complex. In one of his first speeches on this subject, Annan observed that 'Globalization has given hope that human ingenuity and enterprise will take us forward into a new golden age, but serious development challenges remain ... The United Nations and the private sector can and must work together to bring 60 per cent of the world's population into the market.'[1] Annan's words are an excellent place to start any debate.

Globalization and specifically the activities of global companies in the developing world do pose some serious questions. There are still some in business who would dismiss the anti-globalization agenda as, at best, of marginal relevance to their 'bottom line'. However, the sceptics should consider the impact of the emerging anti-globalization agenda on the reputation of business. In recent years, public concern over the environment, human rights and ethical issues has affected a wide range of household name companies such as Nike, Monsanto, Gap, Disney, BP and Shell. In this new communications era, consumer boycotts, campaigns by non-governmental organizations (NGOs) and political pressure are all facts of business life. The 24-hour world of the Internet means that local campaigns in one small corner of the developing world can become the latest big NGO crusade in the UK or the USA, literally overnight.

It is, however, important to understand that companies such as Shell have not begun to change the way they do business simply because they are worried about their reputation. When Shell decided over five years ago to embrace the concept of sustainable development, the reaction from many in both the NGO and investment communities was cynicism, even ridicule. For some, the decision to embark on a series of annual reports detailing Shell's commitment to social, environmental and ethical responsibility was the worst form of 'greenwash', forced on unwilling senior executives by events in Nigeria and the Brent Spar saga. Frankly, any company can produce a glossy report full of vague aspirations, value statements and distant environmental and social targets. But for companies to retain their credibility, they must ensure that the aspirations and the rhetoric are matched by real change in management structures and decision-making and take positive steps to ensure that the vision is translated into action on the ground.

For Shell, the five-year evolution of the Shell Report has taken the publication from a vehicle setting out Shell's core values and general aspirations to a clear, coherent and detailed statement of the business case for sustainable development. This imperative includes the need to attract and motivate top talent, reducing risk through a greater understanding of stakeholder concerns, anticipating and developing new markets, for example in cleaner fuels, attracting more loyal customers and reducing costs through eco-efficiency. On attracting top talent, for example, it is clearly the case that the best graduates increasingly want to work with companies that take their environmental, social and ethical responsibilities seriously. It is these complementary and overlapping drivers that are helping Shell both to optimize current business and to gain new business opportunities. Far from being a drag on business performance, sustainable development is helping Shell to earn its 'licence to grow' and to break new ground in the development of new technologies and new markets.

It would be easy to say that everything in the garden is rosy, but in fact there is much to do. Shell is constantly striving to meet the legitimate expectations of local and international stakeholders and to improve year on year our ethical, environmental and social performance. We do not pretend that we have all the answers or that we get it 100 per cent right every time. We do, however, strive to improve our performance against the backdrop of serious and mounting concern over the impact of globalization, particularly in the developing world. Three of the many legitimate concerns of the anti-globalization movement are particularly worthy of comment.

First, the gap between the 'rich North' and the 'poor South' continues to grow. Conservative estimates suggest that approximately 1.3 billion people live on less than $1 a day. Critics of globalization claim that the activities of international financial institutions such as the World Trade Organization, as well as of individual companies, are adding to the marginalization of the world's poorest nations. Without significant reform, ambitious international development targets of halving global poverty by 2015 are destined to fail.

Second, globalization is blamed for the rise of a global monoculture that is literally suffocating local cultures and local diversity by seeming to impose Western products and services. There is a sense of crushing uniformity about the imposition of brand in inappropriate places. Naomi Klein's *No Logo* has focused international attention on the power of the global brand and its potential consequences for local markets, particularly in the developing world.[2]

Third, globalization is blamed for the exploitation of cheap and even child labour and natural resources in developing countries. Big companies are accused of exporting jobs to cheap-labour regions. Environmentalists claim that multinationals get away with polluting sites in the developing world, where local legislation may set minimal standards of protection and where stakeholder pressures may be non-existent. As Dame Anita Roddick, the founder of The Body Shop, puts it, for global business 'each country is just another pit stop in the race to an ever-improved bottom line'.[3]

For good measure, Dame Anita also claims that 'when business can roam from country to country with few restrictions in its search for the lowest wages, the loosest environmental regulations and the most docile and desperate workers, then the destruction of livelihoods, cultures and environments can be enormous'.[4] This is what multinationals are accused of. What is the Shell perspective on this and how does it affect our work, day to day?

First, I am proud to be working for a truly global company that takes its environmental, social and ethical responsibilities seriously. Part of taking these issues seriously involves making written contributions such as this one and discussing these issues openly and transparently. Companies can no longer argue that they are a private company whose only responsibility is to their shareholders. That line is best left to a dwindling band of companies that cling to the old notion that 'the business of business is business'.

For Shell, the way in which we do business is critically important to both our reputation and, more importantly, our long-term prosperity. Our day-to-day business is informed by an overriding commitment to seven sustainable development principles, spanning our economic, social and environmental performance. In addition, Shell was the first energy company to write support for human rights into its business principles, and the first to produce a detailed human rights practical guide for staff to raise awareness of key human rights issues.

Principles lack real meaning unless they are seen to be informing day-to-day business activities and strategic direction. This is why the latest Shell report is crammed full of case studies that highlight our sustainable development principles in action. Two projects serve as good examples of the Shell approach. First, the Malampaya gas pipeline project in the Philippines will make a major contribution to reducing the Philippines' dependence on imported fuels, and has enormous macro political and economic consequences. The project also has considerable local implications and only went ahead after detailed environmental and social studies with local stakeholders. This led, for example, to the rerouting of the pipeline to avoid environmentally and culturally sensitive areas. Second, in Malaysia, the world's first major Shell Middle Distillate Synthesis (SMDS) plant is turning gas into ultra-clean liquid fuels. Shell believes that SMDS fuels can play a significant role in addressing urban air quality issues throughout Asia, without the need for costly new infrastructure.

This last example of SMDS also raises a wider issue of importance to Shell. We are not embracing a commitment to sustainable development out of the goodness of our heart. Shell sees sustainable development as making good business sense in helping to differentiate us from our competitors and providing competitive business advantage. In a carbon constrained world, Shell believes that customers, governments and other stakeholders will want to do business with companies that are seeking imaginative and efficient lower carbon solutions, and who are working to deliver positive solutions. In other words, they will want to do business with companies that are part of the solution, not the problem. There is clearly a competitive advantage to be gained from being 'first among the pack' in developing cleaner fuels and providing greater customer choice, rather than waiting until domestic or international regulation forces change.

Another area where Shell sees a long-term competitive advantage in adopting a principled approach to business is in dealing with bribery and corruption. Due to our very clear and principled stand on corruption, there is no doubt that Shell companies have missed out on contracts in recent years. There have been occasions when we have been unable to conclude an agreement because, at the last moment, a demand for 'consultancy fees' from intermediaries connected with the government has been made. More positively, in some recent dealings with governments that have not always been transparent in the past, officials have made clear their insistence on open dealings with us without the use of intermediaries. We believe that our principled approach is helping to have a positive impact, not only on the business world, but on governments as well.

This experience allows us to understand the impact of globalization and the dilemmas it poses at the local level and reveals two important facts.

First, the forces of globalization are inevitable and of potentially positive benefit to both the developed and the developing worlds. In the energy industry, global companies such as Shell are opening up enormous opportunities to build a more sustainable future based on lower carbon gas and the long-term exploitation of renewables such as wind, biomass and solar PV. Kofi Annan has argued that the industrialized nations need to bring 60 per cent of the world's population into the energy market, but this can only be achieved throughout the developing world by the more rapid development of hydrocarbon resources, principally gas and associated fuel products. This does not rule out the long-term prospects for renewables, but it is vital not to exaggerate their pace of growth and potential contribution to the world's energy mix over the next 20 years.

Second, it is important to meet head-on the argument that global companies have more power than many countries in the developing world and that they use that power to exploit local human and natural resources. Of all the arguments advanced by our critics, this is the most simplistic, and it is just plain wrong. Anita Roddick again summarizes this view when she says: 'only 27 countries have a turnover greater than the combined sales of Shell and Exxon . . . So in terms of power and influence, you can forget the Church and forget politics too. There is no more powerful institution in society than business.'[5] This is an absurd point of view: of course, we have huge responsibilities that go with our global role, but to suggest, for example, that throughout Latin America, or Africa, or Asia, or Europe we have more power than individual governments and state institutions is at best misleading and, at worst, actually risks letting countries and politicians off the hook.

Robin Aram, Shell's Vice President for External Relations, recently commented: 'it is also necessary for governments and societies to act in the awareness that economic liberalisation is not enough. There is a clear need to encourage saving and investment, to educate people and to strive for social inclusion together with political and economic stability.' Global companies such as Shell can play their part in working to advance this agenda in individual countries, but the public in general need to keep a sense of perspective about the power of companies to force countries to adopt high environmental, social and ethical standards. It is the role of multinationals to transfer best business practice, to train staff to the highest standards, and to work harder to lift people up. It is important to note that this role should not extend to companies acting as some sort of corporate nanny filling the health, education and quality of life gap left by unwilling governments or societies at an early stage of economic development. Two issues illustrate the situation very clearly. Nigeria continues to demonstrate the inherent tensions between rapid economic development and ensuring that all sections of society benefit from the increased wealth that this can bring. There is much community agitation for greater and rapid development of the Niger Delta. This has led to a highly volatile situation, but this is not surprising. The expectations of the 7 million people living in the Niger Delta remain high, and so they should. They have yet to benefit in a significant way from the oil wealth generated from their land.

Just one of the many questions this raises is the extent to which international companies can use their influence to ensure a fairer distribution of the economic cake. Companies can and do urge greater attention to these issues, but it is not for Shell or any other company to dictate to the Nigerian government a specific course of action. Furthermore, the Nigerian government is improving its act, as it has set up the Niger Delta Development Commission to oversee socio-economic development. At last and after far too long, government funds have begun to flow to the oil-producing states. As part of its ongoing work, the Commission held a Niger Delta Summit in 2001, partly funded by Shell, and commissioned a master development plan for the region. For our part, SPDC (the wholly Shell-owned Nigerian subsidiary) spent more than $50 million in 2001 on community development projects, and a number of international agencies, including the World Bank and UNICEF, were involved in external reviews of the company's activities as part of the World Bank's 'Partners for Development' initiative. Despite these initiatives, Shell remains conscious that the world and the people of the Niger Delta are still watching and that the company cannot afford to be complacent in continuing to address local development issues with our Nigerian partners. It is worth repeating that there are clear limits to the action that companies can take.

The second example concerns child labour. Today, the youngest Shell employee anywhere in the world is 16 and lives in the USA. Like all ethical issues, child labour is not always as simple as we might like to assume. Sometimes, international companies have to deal with local circumstances that throw up very difficult choices. In Brazil, for example, energy companies are required by law to add 15 per cent ethanol from local sugar cane production to fuel. The problem with this law is that, in Brazil, sugar cane is largely harvested by children. In order to mitigate this unhappy situation, Shell went back to the government in the late 1990s and said that all of us – government, energy companies, sugar cane producers and communities – have a responsibility to deal with this situation. In 1999, Shell Brazil was awarded the title of 'Child Friendly Company' for its pioneering work in discouraging the use of child labour in the production of sugar cane alcohol. Shell Brazil has introduced a clause in its contracts with distillers forbidding the use of child labour and asking them to respect our principles. This followed a broad debate with NGOs, local government and distillers to find ways of helping families whose children work in the sugar cane fields. New funds have been set up to educate the children who would otherwise have no option but to go to work to support their families.

This raises the important issue of dealing with social, ethical and environmental standards as they are, not how we would wish them to be. Or to put it another way, at what stage does Shell replace positive engagement in a country with a decision to pull out of individual regimes such as Burma? Are there any other 'no go' areas? The honest answer is that there are no easy answers. Each case is judged and re-judged on its own merits. We are well aware that there are many people both within and outside Shell who will not always agree with our investment or business decisions.

For example, Shell has growing interests in Iran from oil exploration to petrochemicals and liquefied natural gas. Some people will argue that Iran is a country we should steer clear of given its poor human rights record. However, Shell is of the firm view that, at this stage, international trade will help the process of democratization in that country and that the opening up of Iran to major international investment is inevitable in the long term. In South Africa, as I mentioned earlier, we were hounded to pull out along with other high-profile UK and US companies. We stayed on the basis that we could provide an island of business decency and normality and that our working conditions and practices could in a very small way offer at least a glimpse of what a post-apartheid South Africa could achieve.

This article should give a flavour of the many ethical problems that a company such as Shell faces almost every day. We are proud of our record on these issues but we are not complacent. As I keep reminding employees in Shell UK, we can never afford to rest on our laurels and assume that what may satisfy stake-holders one year will set high enough standards for the stake-holders of the future. It is also important that we do not overstate the role that global companies can play in contributing to sustainable development and advancing ethical and social goals. Governments and international institutions must surely continue to have the primary responsibility for establishing ethical frameworks and in working to deliver social development for their citizens. On corruption, for example, individual governments have a clear responsibility to provide a level business playing field that does not place ethical companies at a disadvantage.

So, if governments and international institutions and, to a lesser extent, companies and NGOs are the key institutional drivers of these issues, what about the role of the individual? I began this article by emphasizing that there is no distinction between my life as a parent, a Christian, a member of the local community and a Shell employee. Equally, I don't stop being a Shell employee when I spend time working with the Lambeth Education Action Zone to help disadvantaged young people, which is literally just a stone's throw from Shell's headquarters. Lambeth is the reception area for many of the poorest immigrants who come to the UK. The challenges of language, culture, employment and poverty are as great in Lambeth as anywhere in the country. It is an important issue locally and not that different to the one you find in many countries. The world and many of the world's problems are literally on our doorstep. Our concern, our conscience and our commitment start here.

Notes

1. Delivered at the World Economic Forum in Davos, Switzerland, 1 February 1997. See http://www.un.org/News/Press/docs/1997/19970131.sgsm6153.html
2. Naomi Klein, *No Logo: Taking Aim at the Brand Bullies* (Flamingo, London, 2000).
3. Anita Roddick, *Business as Unusual: The Triumph of Anita Roddick* (Thorsons, London, 2000), p. 7.
4. Anita Roddick, *Business as Unusual*, p. 14.
5. Anita Roddick, *Business as Unusual*, p. 14.

Part II

4

Getting the Social Relations Right: Towards an Integrated Theology and Theory of Development

MICHAEL WOOLCOCK

In the debate about globalization, the theology and theory of international development are usually considered separate from, and even antithetical to, one another. Participants often work from different epistemological assumptions in their approach to the issues; they lack a language and framework for generating a richer dialogue between them. It need not be so. This chapter attempts to outline the basis for a more integrated approach to the theology and theory of development, doing so on the basis of a unifying theme that centres on 'getting the social relations right'. To my mind, the nature and extent of relationships between people has a major bearing on the quality of life and opportunities they enjoy, and, concomitantly, poverty is a manifestation of failed social relationships. In recent years, theologians and development scholars have made similar claims, but have made them independently. This chapter seeks, therefore, to identify and synthesize their complementarities.

A theology of development

Much theological reflection on globalization, development and poverty begins and ends with a stress on the importance of justice. Micah's timeless counsel to 'act justly and to love mercy and to walk humbly with your God' (Micah 6.8) is frequently invoked. Indeed, a concern for justice is taken as the basis for spirited (and proper) campaigns for freeing political and religious prisoners, forgiving foreign debt and decrying global economic inequalities. Justice, however, is a necessary but insufficient condition for development and poverty reduction. This is for two reasons. First, it largely focuses on removing negatives rather than inspiring the construction of positives. Second, even in a putatively 'just' – that is to say, fair, transparent and equitable – world, everyone could still live Hobbesian lives that are poor, nasty, brutish and short. A more complete theology of development needs an additional element.

'Vision' and 'hope' are possible candidates, but I prefer the idea of 'glory', as embodied in St Irenaeus of Lyons' assertion 1,800 years ago that 'the glory of God is a human being fully alive'.[1] I submit that nothing more systematically precludes people from being 'fully alive', and thus living a life more approximating to God's glorious image in which all of us are made, than grinding poverty. That does not mean that the poor can't or don't live meaningful lives (they can and do), nor that rich people are morally superior (they aren't), nor that enduring poverty in an age of plenty is a function of the poor's 'culture' or 'backward' behaviour (it isn't), nor that more widespread prosperity will necessarily come without other social, psychological or environmental costs (it probably won't). It does mean, however, that we can confidently assert that poor countries and poor individuals will be better off and 'more glorious' when they are less poor.

Glory makes regular appearances in popular conversation during the Olympic Games and the various World Cups; it is the title of one of the best films of 1989, of America's flag (Old Glory) and Britain's popular creed (the 'land of hope and glory'). Most of us can join the singer Bruce Springsteen in fondly recalling some period in our life as our 'Glory Days'.

Glory is also a distinctively and deeply religious word. It has featured prominently throughout the Church's history in its liturgies, prayers, hymns and songs. But what does it actually mean to fulfil the oft-repeated injunction to 'give God glory'? There are three major traditions we can call on to help us answer this, and together these traditions capture some of the most important truths regarding the distinctiveness, originality and power of the Christian message, particularly as it pertains to understanding, and thus responding to, the scourge of poverty.

Biblical images of glory

The most enduring image of glory from the Old Testament is probably that of Moses receiving the Ten Commandments, and the pillar of cloud and fire ('the glory of God') that accompanies the Israelites as they trek through the wilderness. Similar themes surround the Gospel story of the transfiguration. A third theme, also from the New Testament, is that of 'judgement day', the end of history when God will appear 'in glory' to judge the living and the dead, separating the sheep from the goats, the righteous from the unrighteous.

These three images of glory are important, but at first brush it is hard for most of us to get excited about them; indeed, if this is our only view of glory, their remoteness from our everyday experience explains in part why glory is so rarely discussed. But those who wrote our scriptures, creeds and hymns thought it important, presumably, because it emphasizes that our understanding of God cannot be contained within our minds, our theological approximations or our houses of worship. This is illustrated, for example, in the book of Job, in the Psalms (which express the wonder and greatness of God), in the book of Isaiah, and in the New Testament (with its reminders that God is and can do more than we can possibly imagine). So glory in what we might call the Grandeur Tradition of Scripture is about God's otherness, omnipotence and omnipresence. If the Grandeur Tradition is not something we can fully comprehend, then perhaps that is exactly as it should be: God is God, and we are not.

Glory has at least two other uses in Scripture, however, and these can be seen most vividly in Luke's Gospel, which graphically depicts God's special concern for marginalized people: women and children, the sick, the poor, the outcast. Luke is the sole source for two of Jesus' best-known stories, namely the Good Samaritan and the Prodigal Son, his masterpiece. Luke's goal was to demonstrate Jesus' embodiment of what Marcus Borg (1995, 1997) aptly calls God's 'radical egalitarianism' of love, grace and compassion – that being in right relationship matters more than obeying rigid, divisive rules.

Luke's Gospel refers to glory more than any of the other Gospels. While it is the source of some of the most enduring images of glory we have in the Grandeur Tradition – those associated with Jesus' birth and transfiguration, for example – its theology of glory goes further than this tradition and is more comprehensive. Having just turned down the devil's offer to trade 'the world and its glory' in exchange for worshipping him, Luke's Gospel has Jesus present his so-called 'inaugural address' – the dramatic speech in the synagogue in which he announces the purpose of his mission:

> 'The Spirit of the Lord is on me, because he has anointed me to preach good news to the poor. He has sent me to proclaim freedom for the prisoners and recovery of sight for the blind, to release the oppressed, to proclaim the year of the Lord's favour.' (Luke 4.18–19; Isaiah 61.1–2)

Later, in the run-up to Jesus' triumphant entry into Jerusalem in Luke 19, we get a barrage of short, concluding vignettes demonstrating both the message Jesus was trying to convey and the means he sought to realize it. All of these stories and events are about Jesus' entry into people's lives, relationships and situations – Zacchaeus, the ten blind men, the rich young ruler, and the story of the lost coin and of the persistent widow, among others.

This tradition of glory – let's call it the Grace Tradition – runs through both the Old and the New Testaments, but it is Luke who makes it the central theme of his Gospel. The Grace Tradition has a distinctive place within the Christian faith: it defines its very heart and is the basis for its sense of mission. God is glorified, says Luke, when we become participants in the process of moving people towards being in right relationship with themselves, with each other and with God himself. God may be 'out there', as the Grandeur Tradition reminds us, but he is also intimately concerned with what happens 'right here, right now'.

Glory, then, refers to God's grandeur and grace, but there is also a third tradition, which I will call the Gratitude Tradition.

Luke 19 concludes with Jesus' entry into Jerusalem. The people hail this entry as a triumphant occasion, still wanting and expecting military and political glory, not God's glory as Jesus has demonstrated it to them time and again. Even his closest disciples let him down: James and John ask to be honoured by getting seats at God's right and left hand; faced with a threat when soldiers come to arrest Jesus, Peter slashes off a soldier's ear and later denies having had any association with Jesus at all.

The Gratitude Tradition refers to our response to what God has done, is doing and will do in our lives. Sometimes singing songs of praise and adoration is appropriate, as demonstrated frequently in the Psalms. But 'giving glory to God' is equally a matter of humility, quietness, honesty and thankfulness. Luke captures this in the story of the ten healed of leprosy, in chapter 17. All the lepers cry out to be cured, and Jesus duly sends them off to show themselves to the priests. All ten are healed, but only one, a despised Samaritan, throws himself at Jesus' feet in thankfulness.

> 'Where are the other nine?' Jesus asked. 'Was no-one found to return and give praise to God except this foreigner? . . . Rise, and go; your faith has made you well.' (Luke 17.17–19)

The motive behind the expression of gratitude matters more than the expression itself. In Luke 18, in the parable of the Pharisee and the tax collector, both give thanks to God, but the former uses the occasion to trumpet his adherence to the rules and his distance from the outcasts, while the latter pleads with God to restore his life, offering only his humility and surrender. The glory lies with those who realize their need for God, not with those whose gratitude is intended to glorify themselves. 'For everyone who exalts [glorifies] himself will be humbled,' Jesus concludes, 'and he who humbles himself will be exalted' (Luke 18.14).

Glory, then, is about God's grandeur and grace, and our gratitude. Glory makes such frequent appearances in Scripture, hymns and the creeds because it tells us something of who God is (grandeur), what he is like and desires for the world (grace), and how people can respond (gratitude). The Grandeur, Grace and Gratitude Traditions need to be seen as a whole in order to grasp the full meaning of each. Otherwise we join Jesus' followers in missing the full picture of what glory – indeed, Jesus' very life and ministry – signifies.

God has a special bias for the poor, the marginalized, the disenfranchised, as Luke so powerfully and dramatically reminds us; there can be little glory where there is destitution and exclusion, because they are both symptomatic and a cause of estranged social relations. In the following section, I shall explore the extent to which these theological ideas resonate with those in the recent academic and policy literature on development.

A theory of development

To what extent do the major academic theories of development, and the policy prescriptions to which they give rise, take seriously the notion that the nature and extent of social relationships 'matter' for understanding the plight of the poor and the outcast? The answer: a lot more than most people of faith, as well as many academics themselves, recognize.

One can discern five significantly different perspectives on social relationships in the social-scientific literature on development as it has evolved over the past 50 years. These perspectives stress, respectively, the idea that social relations are (a) an obstacle, (b) epiphenomenal, (c) necessarily beneficent, (d) irrelevant, and (e) both a potential asset and a constraint. The first perspective, characterized by the prevailing development theory of the 1950s and 1960s – modernization theory – was an understanding that social relations in poor countries and communities were in some sense a problem to be overcome. When modernization theorists sought to explain the absence or the 'failure' of capitalism, the focus was on social relations as obstacles (Moore, 1997: 289).

Development theory began to fragment in the 1970s, and the intellectual dominance and putative coherence of modernization theory gave way to two parallel but distinct perspectives. The non-economic social sciences (and some left-wing economists) began to support the arguments of dependency and world-systems theorists, who held social relations among corporate and political elites to be a primary mechanism of capitalist exploitation.[2] For writers from this perspective, the social characteristics of poor countries and communities were defined almost exclusively in terms of their relations to the means of production and the inherent antipathy between the interests of capital and labour. Development, in the famous phrase of André Gunder Frank (Frank, 1969), was held to be a direct product of the 'underdevelopment' of the Third World. These perspectives essentially viewed social relations as of secondary importance or 'epiphenomenal'. They were the product of class relations, historically and politically constructed.

Such views had a 'micro' counterpart in communitarian perspectives, with their emphasis on the inherent virtue of local communities and the importance of self-sufficiency. Communitarians – whose creed was 'small is beautiful'[3] – struggled to consolidate their claims through either mobilizing a viable political constituency or grounding themselves in a rigorous social theory. Their claims failed to account for the negative aspects of communal obligations and vastly overestimated the virtues of isolationism and self-sufficiency. They also tended towards a romanticism of the past, indulging a nostalgia for times past when the sense of 'community' was allegedly a more effective bulwark against the stresses of modern society (Phillips, 1993). Communitarians can thus be said to hold a naively beneficent view of social relations.

For its part, the economics of development took a decided turn towards neo-classical theories from the early 1970s, achieving the peak of its influence in the 1980s (ably supported by the political philosophies of Reagan and Thatcher) and, in the aftermath of the fall of socialism, the early 1990s. Such approaches assigned no distinctive properties to social relations per se, focusing instead on the strategic choices of rational, self-interested individuals interacting under various constraints. Moreover, groups (including firms) were held to exist primarily for the purpose of lowering the transaction costs of exchange (Williamson, 1975); given undistorted market signals, the optimal size and combination of groups would duly emerge. As such, social relations in the sociological sense were either irrelevant, of merely instrumental importance, or secondary derivatives of the actions of otherwise atomistic, disparate individuals seeking to maximize their welfare.

For the major development theories, then, social relations have been construed as singularly burdensome, exploitative, liberating or irrelevant. The variety of events in the post-Cold War era – from deadly civil wars and the rise of the 'anti-globalization' movement to periodic financial crises and the persistent failure of many post-socialist economies – have, however, changed the intellectual landscape considerably.[4] The twin effect of this process has been to bring social relations back into development theory *and* to further fragment development theory and research. Contemporary social science, it seems, is 'coming together' on *what* should be studied in development just as it simultaneously 'falls apart' regarding *how* to study it, how to interpret empirical findings, and how to respond with more effective strategies.

For the issue of social relations, one of the upshots of these trends is that a steady stream of research is being conducted on it, but in virtual ignorance of what others in related fields are doing. It is beyond the scope of this chapter to elaborate on this in detail,[5] but numerous examples can readily be found, from political economy, household economics, economic sociology and comparative politics. In these, remarkably complementary empirical claims are made that centre on the importance of having dynamic and inclusive social institutions (such as kinship systems, networks and local organizations) *and* high-quality institutions in place to manage economic transitions.

These recent empirical findings have given rise to corresponding policy strategies, which today emphasize an overtly participatory approach to the design, implementation and maintenance of local-level development projects.[6] In Indonesia, for example, projects valued at over $1 billion are being designed along precisely these lines, and are being expanded into the Philippines and Afghanistan. Micro-credit programmes in Bangladesh and India, which extend credit to thousands of small groups of women, conduct their activities entirely without formal contracts, lending on the basis of the strength of hand-shake agreements made among group members. I call this emerging convergence of theological and theoretical views one that emphasizes 'getting the social relations right', in contrast to the insistence of many economic policy-makers to 'get the prices right'.

Conclusion

All the major world religions and moral philosophies implore the rich to share with, or at least show compassion for, the poor. All the problems commence, however, when we try to address the political and administrative realities of acting on that imperative. How, exactly, should the riches of wealthy countries best be shared? Should the 'giving' continue even when the 'receivers' are known to be crooks, or the institutional environment obviously inadequate? To what extent should rich countries be prepared to let industries in which poor countries have a comparative advantage, such as agriculture, encroach upon the livelihoods of their farmers? How might we know which approach is most effective, efficient and fair?

The search for adequate practical responses to these vexing concerns is significantly enhanced when a basic framework can be identified that is consistent with contemporary thinking on the theology and theory of development. Many see these as separate, even mutually exclusive, realms – the first for theologians and churchgoers ('believers'), the second for academics and intellectuals ('thinkers'). But along with Stephen Carter I reject such divisions of intellectual labour, and indeed would be deeply troubled if there were significant discrepancies between the messages coming from both.[7] I think a close reading of both shows encouraging synergies, and thus opportunities for further dialogue and advancement.

The essence of that synergy is summarized in the idea that the theology, theory and indeed practice of development are in essence about 'getting the social relations right'. Persistent poverty is both a symptom and a cause of a world in which the social relations are in some fundamental sense 'wrong'. Living the life that God intends for us all – one in which we more perfectly reflect his glory – will entail a concerted effort by rich, poor and mediators alike to get them 'right'. It is the particular burden of members of faith communities and those who articulate their theology to take up this challenge, but to do so by taking social science seriously, seeing it as part of the solution, rather than as something inherently 'secular', and therefore of secondary importance or, worse, part of the problem. An increasingly integrated world requires an increasingly integrated approach to addressing its most pressing political and moral problem: the persistence of poverty in the context of excessive wealth.

Notes

1. St Irenaeus of Lyons (*c.*130–200), *Against the Heresies* 4.20.7.
2. Dependency theory was primarily concerned with explaining contemporary disparities in national wealth; world-systems theory was a larger and more ambitious project that took on the task of explaining the historical emergence and global spread of capitalism as a way of organizing economic life.
3. Derived from Schumacher (1973).
4. See the contributions of Douglass North (1990), Robert Putnam (1993) and Amartya Sen (1999).
5. See Woolcock (forthcoming) for a more complete discussion of this point.
6. On this see Bebbington *et al.* (forthcoming).
7. Carter (1993). See also Belshaw *et al.* (2001).

References

Bebbington, A., Guggenheim, S. and Woolcock, M. (eds) (forthcoming), *Practical Theory, Reflective Action: Social Capital, Empowerment Strategies and Development Projects at the World Bank.* Oxford University Press, New York.

Belshaw, D., Calderisi, R. and Sugden, C. (eds) (2001), *Faith in Development: Partnership Between the World Bank and the Churches of Africa.* Regnum Books, Irvine, CA; The World Bank, Washington, DC.

Borg, M. (1995), *Meeting Jesus Again for the First Time: The Historical Jesus and the Heart of Contemporary Faith.* HarperSanFrancisco, San Francisco.

Borg, M. (1997), *The God We Never Knew*. HarperSanFrancisco, San Francisco.

Carter, S. (1993), *The Culture of Disbelief: How American Law and Politics Trivialize Religious Devotion*. Basic Books, New York.

Frank, A. G. (1969), *Capitalism and Underdevelopment in Latin America: Historical Studies of Chile and Brazil*. Monthly Review Press, New York.

Moore, M. (1997), 'Societies, Polities and Capitalists in Developing Countries: A Literature Survey', *Journal of Development Studies* 33(3): 287–363.

North, D. (1990), *Institutions, Institutional Change, and Economic Performance*. Cambridge University Press, New York.

Phillips, D. (1993), *Looking Backward: A Critical Appraisal of Communitarian Thought*. Princeton University Press, Princeton, NJ.

Putnam, R. (1993), *Making Democracy Work: Civic Traditions in Modern Italy*. Princeton University Press, Princeton, NJ.

Schumacher, E. F. (1973), *Small is Beautiful: Economics as if People Mattered*. Harper & Row, New York.

Sen, A. (1999), *Development as Freedom*. Random House, New York.

Williamson, O. (1975), *Markets and Hierarchies – Analysis and Antitrust Implications: A Study in the Economics of Internal Organization*. Free Press, New York.

Woolcock, M. (forthcoming), *Situating Social Capital: Getting the Social Relations Right in the Theory and Practice of Economic Development*. Princeton University Press, Princeton, NJ.

5

Preparing for a Great Transformation: Putting Human Rights before Money Rights

ANN PETTIFOR

In developing countries, billions in reserves have been bled out of central banks, billions in asset values have been destroyed, and millions of workers have fallen into poverty and chronic insecurity. Global capital markets have acted as gigantic engines of inequality, transferring wealth from the weak to the strong, from debtors to creditors, wage earners and taxpayers to the holders of paper claims, from productive to financial activity.

Kari Polanyi Levitt, in *The Contemporary Significance of the Great Transformation* (1999)

The new dominance of finance capital

We live today in a global economy dominated once again, as in the 1920s, by international finance capital. According to one estimate, before 1970, 90 per cent of all international transactions were accounted for by trade and only 10 per cent by capital flows. Today, despite a vast increase in global trade, that ratio has been reversed, with 90 per cent of transactions accounted for by financial flows not directly related to trade in goods and services.[1] Most of these flows have taken the form of highly volatile stocks and bonds, derivatives, futures, currency trading and short-term loans. In the early 1980s, the stock of global financial assets was closely related to the stock of 'real wealth', i.e. physical capital, plus human capital, plus accumulated research and development expenditures, used as a proxy to measure the stock of technology and know-how. By 2000, however, the stock of financial assets was almost three times larger than the stock of real productive wealth.[2] By 1992, financial assets from the advanced nations of the OECD (the Organization for Economic Cooperation and Development) totalled $35,000 billion – twice the economic output of the OECD in that year. McKinsey and Company predicted that the total financial stock would have reached $53,000 billion by the year 2000 – 'triple the economic output of the OECD economies'.[3]

While campaigners express outrage at the activities of big corporations, they ignore the activities of a much bigger, far more powerful, but almost invisible sector of the global economy – the finance sector.

The changes wrought to the global economy – including the shift from the dominance of industrial capital to finance capital – did not come about 'naturally' or 'spontaneously', as is often suggested.[4] Nor were they the result of technological advances. As Eric Helleiner has shown, they were instead the direct result of major changes in the economic policies of Western governments, in particular the deregulation of global financial markets.[5] These governments are made up of elected and, on the whole, accountable politicians – not abstract economic forces.

To understand these changes, we need to note one important fact about the global economy. Between 1945 and 1970, the United States and its Western allies were major exporters of capital. From 1970 (i.e. post-Vietnam War) until the present day, the US and the UK have become major importers of capital – to finance their growing and, in the case of the US, unsustainable trade deficits and other foreign liabilities. This reversal in financial flows is at the heart of the transformation that has come to be called 'globalization'.

Today the US requires $4 billion a day to finance its deficit and foreign liabilities.[6] To finance its deficit, and to do so without structurally adjusting its economy (by lowering living standards), the US must access foreign savings or capital – in foreign capital markets. In the early 1970s, these markets were still regulated by 'capital controls' put in place and agreed by Western leaders under the terms of the 1944 Bretton Woods Conference, in reaction to the deregulation of the 1920s and 1930s – deregulation widely held to be responsible for the 1930s financial crash.

But in the 1970s, the US government, with its elected politicians in the lead, began to bring pressure on other governments to dismantle these controls so that the US could more easily obtain finance for its deficit. The UK government, supported by the City of London, was only too willing to act as mediator between the indebted US and international capital markets.

The deregulation of capital markets, through the lifting of exchange controls, greatly eased US access to foreign capital markets. But at the same time these changes, and the vast sums of money they set loose, elevated the role that these markets and their major players now exert in the global economy. Financial market-makers gradually expanded that role, so that today the finance sector is dominant.

The finance sector is mainly made up of creditors and investors; but it also includes speculators and gamblers who take risks in stockmarkets, in derivatives and in trading 'futures'. Creditors can include private, corporate or banking creditors; but also public creditors, like governments and the 'multilateral' bodies – institutions such as the International Monetary Fund (IMF) and the World Bank. Through these institutions, richer governments cooperate to lend funds on economic conditions that extend beyond normal banking conditions – enabling government lenders, and their agents at the IMF, to exercise undue influence on weaker economies.

The growth of the finance sector from 1970 onwards ensured the dominance of creditors and investors in the global economy, and this in turn influenced policy-making. In broad terms, policy-making shifted from policies that were essentially inflationary to a range of policies that were deflationary. Inflationary policies, as anyone with a mortgage will know, and as Keynes so cogently argued, transfer assets from creditors to debtors. Deflationary policies achieve the reverse: they transfer assets from debtors to creditors.

From the 1970s onwards, governments and international financial institutions, responding to pressures from creditors/bankers, began to impose deflationary policies on their own people, and also on developing countries. These policies were/are dominated by bankers' concerns (a) for 'price stability' – that is, the need to maintain a stable value for goods, labour and services; and (b) for 'balanced (government) budgets', in case government borrowing 'crowds out' the private sector. Yet overemphasizing price stability can lead to other economically detrimental side-effects. Deflationary policies ensure that government borrowing is limited by cuts in public spending. Cuts in government spending lead to lower levels of demand within the economy, which is followed by falling prices. Falling prices affect profitability adversely, which leads to plant closures and rising unemployment. Increased unemployment, in turn, lowers wages, reducing costs. People consume less, so imports fall, affecting incomes of other trading nations. This can lead, as it did in the 1930s and threatens to again, to a global deflationary spiral. Bankers and creditors are on the whole blind to this threat, as their major concern is with lower wages, lower prices and lower government borrowing – all outcomes which they believe protect creditor assets.

But the evidence shows that central bankers had only a partial concern with inflation. While deflating prices in one part of the economy, they presided over, and can be said to have encouraged, asset price inflation, which enriched those with assets – the rich. Central bankers like Alan Greenspan refused to apply the brakes on this particular inflationary spiral (e.g. by raising interest rates) despite warnings from Milton Friedman, the renowned University of Chicago Nobel laureate.[7]

The IMF, acting on behalf of its dominant shareholders, which are Western governments, has been an important vehicle for the transmission of deflationary policies around the world. The ultimate purpose of these 'structural adjustment policies' is to protect the value of creditor assets. These policies are imposed via the economic conditions attached to lending or debt cancellation. In other words, highly indebted nations have had little choice but to adopt policies that deflate their economies, lower living standards and facilitate the extraction and transfer of assets from the debtor nation to its creditors. In the 1920s, similar deflationary economic policies were applied in order to stabilize currencies under the gold standard to guarantee debt service to foreign bondholders. However, the result, particularly in the UK, was a prolonged economic slump accompanied by the dismissal of public servants, reduced wages and persistent unemployment.

Much the same happens today. Instead of the gold standard we have the euro, which is used across Europe – a uniform currency applied to economies that differ fundamentally. While bankers, creditors and investors welcome such a uniform currency across broad markets, individual economies buckle under the strains it imposes. European bankers heavily influenced politicians in the design of the euro and ensured that the misnamed 'Stability and Growth Pact' was linked to adoption of the new currency by individual countries. Under the terms of the Stability and Growth Pact, overseen by unaccountable bankers and bureaucrats, governments that do not adopt essentially deflationary policies are penalized. This happens even if governments are given democratic mandates to stimulate demand and reduce unemployment. It is widely accepted that the constraints of the pact are exacerbating rising unemployment and recession in the engine room of Europe's economy, Germany.

In developing countries, finance ministers, officially or unofficially, agree to the 'dollarization' of their economies. As a result their people adopt, formally or informally, a foreign currency, and the interest rates linked to that currency. While widespread use of a stable currency like the dollar is attractive to foreign creditors and investors, or to those who can afford a Western lifestyle, it may not suit the interests of most of the people of the developing country.

The rise or fall of interest rates associated with these currencies, and of the value of the currency itself, is subject to the vagaries of a quite different, much richer economy, and to decisions made far away in New York, by the US Federal Reserve. Alan Greenspan and the board of the Federal Reserve make up an institution with no accountability to people in developing countries like Ecuador. So the Fed. may decide to raise interest rates to curb inflationary pressures in the US, or to attract foreign capital, just at a time when interest rates need to be lowered in Ecuador to encourage investment, and to enable farmers to borrow to buy seeds.

While the value of the dollar may rise, mainly because of flows of capital into the US, these flows of capital may not be heading for Ecuador. Nevertheless the exporters of Ecuador will find the price of their exports fixed in a currency that over-values the exports. They will be expected to compete with capital-rich US exporters in international commodity markets. Under these circumstances they will most likely fail, and the country, as a whole, will suffer. Once again, bankers and creditors, including the IMF, are blind to these developments, concerned only with stable currencies that preserve the value of creditor assets across international boundaries.

Economic policies that placed human rights at their centre, and not just the interests of international bankers and creditors, would require a more diverse range of currencies, to reflect diverse regional, national and local conditions.[8]

Debt as a constant threat to economic stability and human rights

Central to our planned global economy (planned by institutions like the Bank for International Settlements, the IMF, and the finance ministries of the big G7 economies), and dominated by finance capital, is the powerful lever of debt. Debt acts as the key mechanism for the transfer of wealth from weak to strong; from debtor nations to international creditors; from taxpayers and wage earners to the holders of paper claims; from productive to financial activity.[9] Without the leverage of debt, IMF policy-makers, bankers and creditors would not be able to intervene in the design of economic policy, nor to impose the deflationary policies and the deregulation of capital markets that are essential to ensure such transfers.

The new dominance of creditors in the global economy has led, since the late 1970s, to a massive expansion of credit and an equivalent growth in household, corporate and sovereign debts.[10] One glaring example of overindebtedness is the economy of Argentina. Other important economies that are overindebted include the US, Indonesia, Turkey, Pakistan, Brazil, Russia and Nigeria. Of these only the US has, until now, been able to discount the pressures of creditors and maintain a degree of policy autonomy, despite the fact that, between 1999 and 2002, the net indebtedness of the US to the rest of the world increased from $784 billion to $2,387 billion.

Argentina's long history of economic dominance by foreign creditors has skewed its economy towards their interests, and not towards balanced development of the economy as a whole, or of its people. As a result it has not been possible for Argentina to emerge from a pattern of boom, bust and austerity, or from a predictable cycle of political repression and corruption associated with such economic cycles.[11]

Anarchy parading as prosperity

Here in Europe there is very little mention of Argentina's crisis – the public have little awareness of the huge dangers lurking in the global economy – because the anarchy of the international financial system currently parades as prosperity and freedom, as Peter Warburton so rightly argues.[12] Absorbed by our highly demanding rates of consumption, and cushioned by levels of affluence unprecedented in history, we in the West care little for what is happening in the enchanted forest of international finance.

But there are spooks in the anarchic global financial forest – a forest that has been carelessly, if deliberately, cultivated, deregulated and then allowed to run riot by respected central bankers like Hans Tietmayer, Eddie George and Alan Greenspan. The 'spooks' attack like bolts of lightning, unexpectedly and out of the blue, as many recent crises show. There is a growing awareness, however, that the deflationary policies of central bankers (such as the Stability and Growth Pact) and the growing, unsustainable debts of households, corporations and sovereign governments pose a major threat to all of us – particularly to those who are lending, investing, consuming and speculating on borrowed money. In a deflationary environment, the prices of labour, commodities and assets fall, often below cost. Interest rates, however, cannot fall below 0 per cent – and so in real terms interest rates remain high. Those with debts find that they cannot sell their assets to obtain revenues to pay off debts, as the value of these assets has collapsed. And the debts, whose relative value increases, are then subject to high interest rates – in real terms.

Structural imbalances and instability

Japan in the 1980s wallowed in the sort of consumption levels we enjoy in Britain today, with investors recklessly chasing rising asset values higher and higher – all on borrowed money. The parallels between Japan then and Britain and the United States today are, in my view, disturbing. We are living through a classic asset bubble, particularly in London; and, as record surges in mortgages show, people are borrowing, often way beyond their means, to finance not only the purchase of assets but also unprecedented levels of consumption. It was just this process of over-borrowing and over-consuming that led to the build-up of unpayable debts in Japan, and caused deep pain and personal loss when the deflation of asset values led banks and companies to collapse because of large debts. Unemployment rose, incomes fell and the economy stagnated.

But while there are parallels between Japan and Britain and the United States, especially in the reckless lending and borrowing that central banks unleashed to finance such consumption and to fuel the asset bubble, there is one big difference. The Japanese have a trade surplus, and can largely finance their own consumption. Both Britain and the United States are running historically high trade deficits – each day the US consumes $1 billion more in imports than it produces in exports – and on the eve of the 2001 general election, Britain announced an extraordinarily high trade deficit – $7.7 billion – of an order that once lost Harold Wilson a general election. And yet news of that announcement, and of the instability and imbalances that it represented, was greeted with a yawn by economic and political commentators.

Britain and the United States are mobilizing – through international borrowing – two-thirds of the world's savings to finance their growing habit of living beyond their means. The United States, which according to the latest census has a population of just 280 million people, has foreign liabilities of about $3,000 billion. The whole of the developing world, including China, Brazil and India, with populations of 5.1 billion people,[13] have foreign debts of only $2,330 billion.[14]

Debt bondage, ethics and Jubilee 2000

In the West, concern about the domination of finance capital over poor countries has been growing, amplified by the international Jubilee 2000 movement. The campaign's guiding principles were grounded in Judaic and Christian biblical ethics on human rights, opposition to usury, and the need for periodic correction to imbalances – the Sabbath and Jubilee principles. The campaign drew on what Chad Myers called the 'Hebrew Bible's vision of Sabbath economics [which] contends that a theology of abundant grace and a communal ethic of redistribution is the only way out of our slavery to the debt system, with its theology of meritocracy and private ethic of wealth concentration'.[15] These principles and ethics have, in turn, resonated with Muslims and other peoples of faith, and with those of no faith at all.

The element of restraint inherent in these Judaeo-Christian ethics stands in marked contrast to the unfettered financial market liberalism that prevails today. One of the most important of these restraints, or forms of regulation, is something we call Sunday. Central to the process of transforming our societies and economies away from a people-centred approach and towards a money-centred approach was the defeat of the concept of Sunday.

Sunday was – and still is in some societies – a form of regulation. For more than 2,000 years, Jewish and then Christian communities and societies were obliged, on the seventh day of each week, to refrain from exploiting the land and each other – to cease consuming. But the principles and ethics of Sunday have now been destroyed, at least in major Western economies. They had to be, to make way for a new set of ethics that places money, rather than people and the environment, at the centre.

Thus we are left with the 24/7 phenomenon – consumption 24 hours a day – made possible through a massively increased rate of exploitation of labour and of land. Indeed, the deregulation of Sunday has helped to establish a climate in which many other forms of deregulation are permissible, meaning that only the fittest are expected to survive.

The need for discipline and regulation of our economy, to ensure that money rights are subordinated to human rights, is why the Jubilee concept has proved so fundamental and so relevant to our heavily indebted 'globalized' economy, as the Jubilee 2000 movement demonstrated. The movement found inspiration in the notion that periodically, once every seven times seven years, society would be automatically obliged to correct imbalances, to end injustices, to cancel debts and to start again. If it were implemented, this principle, along with that of the sabbath, would provide a welcome form of discipline on both lenders and debtors.

Reintroducing forms of regulation that discipline capital and place human rights, rather than money rights, at the centre of human affairs would lead to a new great transformation. But for this to happen, certain conditions are necessary: first, the political will (it was political will that led to the deregulation of capital flows), and second, the need to face reality: that a society based almost entirely on money and market values is not economically, socially, politically or environmentally sustainable. These conditions have yet to prevail in the West, where consumers continue to ignore major economic and political imbalances and injustices and worship feverishly at the temples of MasterCard, Visa and American Express.

The link between debt bondage and ethics – as an issue of public as well as private morality – is, of course, ancient: throughout our history, laws have been promulgated against usury. In England a series of post-Reformation usury laws set maximum rates of legal interest for money-lending, which in 1713 finally settled at 5 per cent. The limitation on interest was to remain operative throughout the early industrial period, being finally abandoned only in 1854.[16] A loan which fell foul of the usury law was unlawful and unenforceable by the lender. Adam Smith did not consider that free market notions justified the lifting of this 'prudent fetter on cupidity'.[17] Until quite recently it was possible for usurers to be excommunicated by the Catholic Church; and usury is still a crime that can be fiercely punished under Islamic shariah law. Attempts over the centuries to legislate against usury reflect ethical concerns about the exploitation of weak and vulnerable debtors by the collective actions of much richer, more powerful creditors.

Punishment through usury is one form of discipline over lenders and borrowers; market forces are another. Within the framework of the current international financial system, sovereign debtors are invariably disciplined for reckless borrowing. Like all dependent debtors they lose policy autonomy, and valuable assets are extracted and transferred out of the country. International lenders, investors and speculators, who may be co-responsible for debt crises, are, on the other hand, protected by billion-dollar 'bail-outs'. These are regularly proffered by the IMF and backed by the US, UK and Japanese treasuries. Such bail-outs effectively protect international creditors from risk, and from the 'wrath' of market forces.

Transformation of global structures

Since 1995, the Jubilee 2000 movement has called for an independent, transparent and accountable process of international insolvency to help reorganize the debt repayments of effectively insolvent countries.[18] Insolvency in our domestic economies operates as a form of discipline on both lenders and borrowers. However, no such discipline exists in the international sphere.

Such a process must be accountable to civil society, both in debtor and in creditor nations. In debtor nations, key stakeholders must have a say in the process of arbitration. Only through such an open process will sovereign debtors be restrained from reckless, and often corrupt, borrowing. And only by imposing the discipline of losses, liabilities and transparency on creditors will Western governments and financiers be restrained from reckless and corrupt lending and from extracting and transferring scarce resources from the poor.

Conclusion

There is a growing consensus, though not among major creditors, that countries with huge populations like Argentina, Turkey, Indonesia, Nigeria, Brazil and Zambia need an orderly process for managing unsustainable debt. However, there is much less public awareness of the enormous threat posed to the stability of the global economy by the activities of undisciplined, protected and greedy creditors, gamblers and investors. On the contrary, their activities – particularly in derivatives trading – are veiled in secrecy, and are effectively protected by highly respected central bankers. In the 1920s, central bankers protected the interests of creditors and investors over the interests of millions of ordinary people, by upholding the austerity and pain associated with a uniform global currency – the gold standard – even as the world plunged into crisis. Today, central bankers and the IMF are once again engaged in protecting the interests of a small number of foreign creditors and investors over the human rights of millions of people. There is now an urgent need for this protectionism to be ended, and for a return to discipline, order and regulation in the international financial system. If we are to prevent another economic crisis on the scale precipitated by the deflationary policies of the 1920s, then it is time to end the domination of money rights over human rights. It is time to re-embed the principles of the Sabbath and the Jubilee in social, economic and environmental relations.

Notes

1. J. A. Kelly, *East Asia's Rolling Crises: Worries for the Year of the Tiger*, Center for Strategic and International Studies (CSIS) Pacific Forum, Pacnet 1 (2 January 1998), quoted in R. P. Cronin, *Asian Financial Crisis: An Analysis of US Foreign Policy Interests and Options* (CSR, 1998).
2. A. Pettifor (ed.), *Real World Economic Outlook* (Palgrave Macmillan, London, 2003), ch. 2.
3. W. Greider, *One World, Ready or Not* (Simon & Schuster, New York, 1997), p. 232.

4. As Karl Polanyi noted, 'there was nothing natural about "*laissez faire*"; free markets could never have come into being merely by allowing things to take their course . . . *laissez faire* itself was enforced by the state'. Quoted by E. Helleiner, 'Globalisation and Haute Finance – déjà vu', in K. McRobbie and K. Polanyi Levitt (eds), *Karl Polanyi in Vienna: The Contemporary Significance of the Great Transformation* (Black Rose Books, Canada, 1999).

5. E. Helleiner, *States and the Reemergence of Global Finance: From Bretton Woods to the 1990s* (Cornell University Press, Ithaca, NY, and London, 1994).

6. R. Greenhill and A. Pettifor, *The US as a HIPC: Heavily Indebted Prosperous Country – How the Poor are Financing the Rich* (Jubilee Research at the New Economics Foundation, London, 2002), http://www.jubileeplus.org/analysis/reports/J+USA7.htm.

7. Pettifor, *Real World Economic Outlook*, Introduction.

8. For more on the issue of currency and monetary reform, see D. Boyle, *The Money Changers: Currency Reform from Aristotle to e-cash* (Earthscan, London, 2002).

9. McRobbie and Polanyi Levitt, *Polanyi in Vienna*.

10. For more detail on global indebtedness, see Pettifor, *Real World Economic Outlook*.

11. A. Pettifor, L. Cisneros and A. Olmos Gaona, *It Takes Two to Tango: Creditor Co-responsibility for Argentina's Crisis and the Need for Independent Resolution* (New Economics Foundation, London, 2001), http://www.jubileeplus.org/analysis/reports/tango_exec.htm. See also A. Pettifor, *Chapter 9/11?* (New Economics Foundation, London, 2002).

12. P. Warburton, *Debt and Delusion: Central Bank Follies that Threaten Economic Disaster* (Allen Lane, London, 1999).

13. Figures as at 2000, in *World Development Indicators, 2002* (World Bank, Washington, DC, 2002).

14. *Global Development Finance 2003* (World Bank, Washington, DC, 2003), p. 221.

15. C. Meyers, 'Jesus' New Economy of Grace: The Biblical Vision of Sabbath Economics', *Sojourners* (July–August 1998), the second of two parts.

16. W. R. Cornish and G. de N. Clark, *Laws and Society in England, 1750–1950* (Sweet & Maxwell, London, 1989), p. 227.

17. A. Smith, *Wealth of Nations* (Random House, London, 1976), pp. 356–8.

18. A. Pettifor and J. Hanlon, *Kicking the Habit* (Jubilee 2000 UK, London, 1999), http://www.jubileeplus.org/analysis/reports/habitfull.htm.

6

Risk, Reward and Responsibility: A Biblical Critique of Global Capital Markets

MICHAEL SCHLUTER

Introduction

For a long time Christians have largely ignored biblical teaching in relation to public life. But we need to rediscover the power and relevance of the biblical vision for society. There are many contemporary systems and structures that facilitate injustice, and as Christians we need to be clear what these are and be concerned to break them. It is important to go beyond the symptoms of distress we see in the world today and look at the underlying causes in the light of biblical teaching. Too often Christians are preoccupied with social action (relieving symptoms), to the neglect of social reform (tackling causes or structures).

There are, I believe, three pillars of global capitalism that we need to be concerned about as Christians: the way in which interest operates, the system of limited liability, and the abandoning of gold-backed currency. All three are essential to the working of global capital markets today. In this chapter I will discuss the first two issues; the third is covered briefly elsewhere.[1] I will address both interest and limited liability from the viewpoint of their effects on relationships, so I shall first set out the reason for this approach.

Christianity is relational

Christianity is a faith in which ultimate reality is relational: the Godhead is shown to be three persons in communication. Similarly, God's relationship with his people is described in terms of a 'covenant' – a long-term, faithful, committed relationship (e.g. Genesis 15.4–5).

Furthermore, the cross of Christ is about reconciliation, another relational term (2 Corinthians 5.17–18). Eternal life is described in John's account of Jesus' words in terms of a relationship, as 'knowing God' (John 17.3). Likewise, righteousness in biblical theology is not primarily about an absence of judicial guilt, but about right relationships – between members of a family or a community.

Ethics in the Bible are essentially about love, which is a relational term relevant to the goals of both the individual and the wider community (Matthew 22.34–40). Christian lifestyle is not primarily concerned with prophetic gifts, financial sacrifice or even being martyred for the faith; it is about the quality of relationships (1 Corinthians 13.1–3).

If relationships are at the very heart of biblical theology, it follows that they are fundamental to the way in which Christians understand and define reality.

Key relational norms in biblical teaching on society

Three key areas of the economic framework need to be considered in the light of biblical relational norms: relationships between owners of property or capital and other citizens, relationships between the state and citizens, and relationships between citizens.

In the first of these areas, the parable of the ten *minas* in Luke 19.12–27 suggests that ownership of capital or property involves taking risks in order to make a return. In part, the risk legitimizes the return. Similarly, the 'neighbour-love' principle requires us to ensure that no harm results from the risks we take in our use of capital or property. So, for example, anyone who has a pension fund needs to consider that God will hold them accountable for how their money is used. If that pension fund is used to finance sex shops, or armaments, or tanks to crush citizens, on the day we meet God face to face it will be no good saying, 'I didn't know, I just put it in the pension fund. I had no control over what happened to the money.' God may reply, 'That capital was yours; it was your responsibility to know how it was used.' Where an asset is ours to use and profit from, we are accountable.

Put very simply, the Bible has a risk theory of capital rather than a labour theory of value. That is to say, while Marx determined the value of products by the amount of labour used to produce them, the Bible determines the legitimate return on capital by the amount of risk taken to achieve it.

Turning to relationships between the state and the citizen, biblical law sets out requirements for protecting property rights, maintaining price stability, and enforcing the rule of law. In a modern context, these roles have been devolved to the state, and they are crucial for economic growth: markets cannot function properly without them. This is not to say that all property distribution today is just, fair or absolute – there may be a need for major land reform in many societies, including our own – but the Bible insists that the market be governed by rules rather than allowing a free-for-all.

Finally, regarding relationships between citizens, biblical law assures the legitimacy of rental contracts (Exodus 22.15; Leviticus 25.8–17) and wage labour (providing that labour is protected – Matthew 20.1–16; Deuteronomy 24.14–15) and, by contrast, the *illegitimacy* of borrowing at interest. It is this last point to which we now turn.

Interest

Biblical teaching on interest

According to the Bible, charging interest on loans is unacceptable to God.[2] Old Testament law clearly states, 'Do not charge your brother interest, whether on money or food or anything else that may earn interest.' This prohibition is comprehensive: the only exception is for loans to foreigners (Deuteronomy 23.19–20). And this passage is by no means an isolated reference: the Old Testament writers spoke about this issue again and again (e.g. Psalm 15.5; Nehemiah 5.1–13; Ezekiel 18.1–18).

The ban on interest in the Old Testament was reinforced by the practice of cancelling debts every seven years (Deuteronomy 15.1–3). So where was the incentive to lend money in the absence of both financial return and the certainty of principal repayment? Deuteronomy 15.9 anticipates this issue. The writer says in effect, 'When the seventh year gets near and all debts are going to be cancelled, don't let this wicked thought come into your mind: "Why should I lend?", because the poor man may cry out to God and you will be held guilty before Him.'

The exemption for loans to foreigners is addressed in the New Testament, where Jesus tells the parable of the talents (Matthew 25.14–30 – similar to that of the ten *minas* in Luke). Here a man who, for fear of his master, buried his one talent in the ground is told, 'You should have put it on deposit at the bank and I would have got it back with interest.' Was Jesus thus allowing interest? No – the servant's excuse, 'Master, I knew that you are a hard man, harvesting where you have not sown and gathering where you have not scattered seed' (v. 24), seems to imply that to take interest on a loan is 'harvesting where you have not sown'. It is the sign of a 'hard' person to simply lend money and walk away with a profit: the risk is minimal, especially if there is collateral on the loan, and no management is required of the lender. By contrast, the other two servants put their master's money to work, thereby supplying management and taking risk.

Elsewhere Jesus says, 'If you lend to those from whom you expect repayment, what credit is that to you? . . . But love your enemies, do good to them, and lend to them without expecting to get anything back' (Luke 6.34–5). There is no mention here of making a profit by charging interest: you have to be willing to lend money and get nothing back. And so, until about 1550, the Christian Church prohibited interest on all loans. After the coming of Christ it seemed inappropriate to treat anyone as a 'foreigner' by charging interest under the Deuteronomy provision.

To understand why the Bible bans interest-based finance, one must consider its effects on various types of relationships.

Effects of interest on lender–borrower relationships

In an interest/debt transaction, risk is not shared equitably between the lender and the borrower. Risk is transferred from the owner of the capital to the borrower and yet the money still belongs to the lender, so the reward goes to one party and the risk is borne largely by the other. (Although it might be said that a lender takes the risk of not getting their money back, in practice today most major loans involve taking collateral, as in the case of a house mortgage.)

Two further effects on lender–borrower relationships can be noted. First, interest marginalizes the relationship by reducing the information needed by the lender. If a friend asks me to lend him £10,000 in return for shares in his company, I will want to know a lot about him before I decide. Does he have integrity of character, does he know his business and how to market it, and am I likely to get my money back? My decision depends on our relationship and on his personal reputation.

By contrast, an interest-based loan contract between a bank and a borrower to buy a house or start a business will be backed with collateral to cover the lender in case things go wrong. The bank may enter the contract without much information about or a longstanding relationship with the borrower. It simply needs to know if the house is worth its valuation, or whether the borrower's pension fund will ensure the bank gets its money if the business goes bust. So, the effect of interest is to minimize the relational preconditions for the financial transaction to take place. From a Christian perspective, however, the financial system ought to reinforce relationships, rather than marginalize them.

Second, interest-based lending can lead to an unhealthy dependence or even a subservient relationship between borrower and lender (Proverbs 22.7). If you owe someone a lot of money, it is almost impossible to bargain on an equal basis or have an equal relationship with them.

Effects of interest on wider social relationships

Arguably, interest-based finance has been a major factor in the growth of Western individualism and the breakdown of community because, as we have seen, it does not require strong relationships in order to work. This is the difficulty with all financial markets. Products have been standardized in such a way that a transaction can occur with minimum knowledge of the other party.

One adverse outcome of the attenuation of lender–borrower relationships in interest-based finance is the facilitation of funding for businesses that savers might deem unethical if they were more aware of how their savings were ultimately being used. Interest-based finance also contributes to the creation of a class of capital owners who are 'reaping where they have not sown' (Matthew 25.26–7), thus undermining the legitimacy of wealth in the public mind. Moreover, capital tends to migrate from depressed regions and communities, and the effects of compound interest lead to the further impoverishment of many low-income countries and low-income families.

Debt finance can cause instability of the economy and of companies as banks and other lenders tend to focus on the same category of borrowers. This can lead to things like asset bubbles, negative equity and insolvency, as the recent over-investment in telecommunications companies has shown.

Finally, interest often leads to concentrations of economic power. Large companies can borrow more cheaply than small companies because they are borrowing larger sums. They are therefore able to grow faster and become even bigger, and end up as companies of enormous size and little effective accountability.

Limited liability

Background and biblical teaching[3]

In 1911 Nicholas Butler, President of Columbia University, wrote these memorable words: 'The limited liability corporation is the single greatest discovery of modern times; even steam and electricity are far less important.'[4]

There are many apparent advantages of limited liability: it encourages the purchase of shares and therefore increases the supply of capital; it helps to ensure, at least in theory, that money goes to those who can use it most efficiently; and it standardizes the risk faced by each investor. The most a person can lose is the value of the shareholding itself. Limited liability makes possible very large companies and the economies of scale that go with them, and, arguably, it spreads wealth. Eleven million people in Britain now own shares; isn't that better than just a few families owning enormous sections of industry?

Furthermore, it would not be possible to have a national stockmarket, let alone an international stockmarket, without limited liability because investors would need so much more information before investing. If every time you put money into a company, you knew you could be liable for whatever debts that company incurred, you would only invest in companies where you had real knowledge of the people involved. Limited liability has the effect of making stockmarkets more like bond markets as a form of low-risk investment.

So, why should we as Christians be concerned about limited liability? Because a debt is an unfulfilled obligation to another person, and Scripture is absolutely clear that debts must be paid (Psalm 37.21; Matthew 18.21–35). It could be argued, however, that a type of limited liability existed in biblical law, since if someone could not pay their debts, they had to sell the leasehold on their land, but only until the next jubilee year. So the borrower's liability was limited in terms of the long-term ownership of the family property. If the money from the sale was not enough to cover the debt, the borrower would go into slavery (a form of bonded service contract), but only for a maximum of six years, after which they would be automatically released. Despite a period of potentially severe hardship, therefore, the debtor knew they would not be in debt for ever.

The situation is very different today. Enron shareholders, for instance, having lost the value of their shareholding, could walk away completely free of any obligation to pay out to Enron's employees, pensioners or suppliers. These debts will remain outstanding for the rest of the creditors' lives because they have no legal redress whatsoever. In the light of biblical teaching, this is not the way for human society to operate.

The principal agent problem

Limited liability also creates the classic case of the principal agent problem in economics: who is ultimately responsible? Shareholders 'own' the company, they can buy or sell it, decide the overall strategy and appoint the directors, but they have no control over, or responsibility for, day-to-day management decisions. In contrast, the directors make the day-to-day decisions but can always claim the outcome was not their fault, but was the result, directly or indirectly, of the overall goals and targets set by the shareholders.

Some of the alarming implications of this division of responsibility are demonstrated by the Clapham rail disaster, in which 35 people died and 113 were injured when a commuter train ploughed into the back of a stationary train near Clapham Junction, south-west of London, in December 1988. Who was ultimately responsible for this tragedy? Was it caused simply by a driver who had not paid careful enough attention to a red signal that morning? Or was the cause much more fundamental, having to do with company policy on safety equipment? For if shareholders want maximum return on capital every three months it is difficult for directors to invest money in areas such as safety because it reduces both the return and the value of the company. Directors could then risk being sacked by shareholders. So who is to blame in cases where under-investment compromises public safety? Surely it is chiefly the company shareholders, who insist on maximizing their profits.

There is another problem: who, in fact, are the shareholders? The shares of many big companies are largely in the hands of pension funds and other financial institutions, and these funds are owned ultimately by anyone with pension savings. Fund managers set targets for the companies in which they invest, requiring maximum returns every three months. So in a sense we as pension holders are ultimately responsible for what companies decide to do, which is highly disturbing. We cannot evade responsibility by pleading distance from the decision-making: it is our money funding the company.

The emphasis on short-term profits that currently drives our financial system is causing much wider distress. In fact, the root cause of the hectic pace of life in Western society today is, I believe, the pressure companies are under to produce short-term returns. The demand from financial institutions, and then from the companies in which they invest, for ever-improving performance means that all their employees are made to work incredibly hard to achieve those outcomes, and public services in turn are driven to deliver results within the same framework. So, if we lament the way in which we are time-poor, we need to blame the way we have structured our financial system, because that is at the heart of the problem.

Relational consequences of limited liability

The effects of limited liability in cases of insolvency can be considered in four relational areas: between directors and creditors, directors and employees, shareholders and creditors, and creditors and banks/authorities.

Creditors are often angry at what they perceive as directors' incompetence and greed, since, in many cases of insolvency, the creditors are ordinary members of the public.

Employees are often angry with directors when insolvency leads to job losses. If wages are not paid, then employees become creditors. A company collapse may also affect employees' pensions.

The shareholder–creditor tension is best illustrated by an example: Carlton and Granada set up ITV Digital in 1998 (as OnDigital) and the new company made a deal worth £315 million with 24 football clubs for the rights to televise their matches for three years. But ITV Digital got into difficulties and Carlton and Granada decided to let the company go into receivership. Because of the limited liability structure, they could simply walk away with no debts. However, the football clubs now faced difficulties, and some smaller clubs that relied on TV income were left facing insolvency – a severe blow for the clubs' local communities. Where is the justice in all that? But the system allows and even facilitates such a situation. (To add insult to injury, several months later the Competition Board allowed Carlton and Granada to merge.)

The fact that governments and banks get paid first in insolvency cases often leaves other creditors embittered. There are often 'insider creditors' who get out before the company goes down.

There are also relational consequences of limited liability even when there is no insolvency. A lack of trust between shareholders and directors can easily develop over issues such as information-sharing, short-termism, directors' pay awards and asset-stripping. Conversely, directors often feel let down if shareholders accept a hostile bid.

Relationship difficulties between shareholders and employees can be caused by shareholder demands for maximum short-term returns, which may lead to the closure of profitable plants and lack of long-term planning and development, which is harmful to employee interests.

As far as relationships between shareholders/directors and the public are concerned, limited liability means that neither shareholders nor directors have a sense of ultimate responsibility for company failures on issues like safety and environmental protection.

The interaction of interest-based finance and limited liability

The interaction of interest-based finance and limited liability has made possible the corporate behemoths we know today, although revolutions in communications and transportation have also played a part. In the West, we tend to assume that companies will adhere to certain ethical norms, given the Christian roots that have influenced our business culture. However, recent developments, as in the case of Enron, have shown that ethical behaviour is not automatic. While giving us a set of guidelines to follow, Scripture is also realistic about the fallenness of human nature, and seeks to mitigate such disasters by promoting diffusion, rather than concentration, of political and economic power.

The enormous scale of corporate interests today has serious consequences for a variety of relationships. Inter-company relationships are harmed when profit allocations are skewed towards the larger players in a transaction, such as when supermarkets deal with small farmers. Relationships between companies and the public suffer particularly in low-income countries, where governments find it difficult to regulate, and are rather beholden to large companies with political leverage. Even in the West, the public often feel disenfranchised, despite consumer protection legislation.

Company–employee relationships are problematic because employees are often powerless pawns as plants are closed, working hours are changed or work locations are moved to another city or even another country.

Personal and wider social relationships between employers and employees are harmed as scale increases lead to wide income differentials. In the largest companies, senior directors often receive remuneration packages several hundred times bigger than those of the average employee.

What can be done?

During the reign of King Ahab, one of the most corrupt rulers in the Bible, there were two different responses to his rule (1 Kings 17—18; 21). Obadiah worked within the system as a close associate of the king, trying to reform the system from the inside; Elijah confronted the system from the outside, saying, 'This has got to be torn down.' We could therefore conclude that there are at least two valid Christian approaches to the problems of global capital markets, depending on where an individual is best placed to challenge the system from – from the inside, as an Obadiah, or from the outside, as an Elijah.

As for specific ways in which the symptoms caused by limited liability and interest-based finance could be tackled, one would be to change the order of payments to creditors in cases of insolvency, so that the Inland Revenue is the last to be paid. The trend towards increasing corporate scale could perhaps be curtailed if companies were required to prove public benefit (or absence of harm) before takeovers were permitted. And tax laws could be reformed to introduce graduated corporate tax rates based on the scale of the enterprise/profits, and to abolish taxes on dividend payments (as pre-tax company profits are already taxed).

Reducing the ubiquity of debt (interest-based) finance will require incentives towards alternative forms of finance that do not rely on interest, such as equity holdings or rental arrangements. Debt finance could also become less attractive if the rules were changed to make interest payments a non-deductible cost for tax purposes, so that debt and equity would be treated on the same basis.

Britain's membership of the EU, and its present level of integration in the 'globalized market', make reforming the concept of limited liability extremely difficult. A move towards increased accountability could cause capital and companies to flee our shores and go elsewhere where they are less accountable. However, we could consider a strategy of giving incentives to companies not to incorporate by making incorporated companies pay higher rates of tax, thus in effect changing corporation tax to 'incorporation tax'. Alternatively, we could make shareholders liable for the first 10 per cent of a company's debts in cases of insolvency, although this could not be done without international agreement and without increasing the transparency in shareholder ownership and identification.

It will be an enormous task to gradually redirect a system that has been going in the wrong direction for 100 years or more. There are no simple answers, but I believe there *are* alternatives. It will take a great deal of research to find them, and commitment to implement them. This, I believe, is the task ahead for Christians wanting to tackle the negative effects of globalization in our world.

Notes

1. Michael Schluter, 'Should Christians Support the Euro?', in Michael Schluter and the Cambridge Papers Group, *Christianity in a Changing World* (Marshall Pickering, London, 2000), p. 159.
2. For a detailed discussion of this issue, see P. S. Mills, *Interest in Interest: The Relevance of the Old Testament Ban on Interest and its Implications for Today* (Jubilee Centre, Cambridge, 1990). See also Paul Mills, 'The Biblical Ban on Interest', in Schluter *et al.*, *Christianity in a Changing World*.

3. For a brief history of limited liability and how it came to be introduced in 1844 and 1855, see M. Schluter, 'Risk, Reward and Responsibility: Limited Liability and Company Reform', *Cambridge Papers* (June 2000).

4. Cited by Aubrey L. Diamond, 'Corporate Personality and Limited Liability', in Tony Ohnial (ed.), *Limited Liability and the Corporation* (Croom Helm, London, 1982), p. 42.

Further reading

Mills, P. and Presley, J., *Islamic Finance: Theory and Practice.* Macmillan, Basingstoke, 1999.

Sykes, A., *Capitalism for Tomorrow: Reuniting Ownership and Control.* Capstone, Oxford, 2000.

Warburton, P., *Debt and Delusion.* Penguin Books, London, 1999.

www.jubilee-centre.org for all *Cambridge Papers* and for Mills, P. S., *Interest in Interest: The Relevance of the Old Testament Ban on Interest and its Implications for Today.* Jubilee Centre, Cambridge, 1990.

7

The Principalities and Powers: A Framework for Thinking about Globalization

TIMOTHY GORRINGE

'Globalization' is a highly contested term, as the non-stop flood of books on the topic shows. I shall use it to designate the integration of all societies, excluding a handful of remaining hunter-gatherer groups, into a global market, and the resulting social, cultural and political changes. Such integration is made possible, first, by the dominance of great corporations, which themselves constitute more than half of the world's largest economies, and, second, by the growth of information technology. This, in turn, has made possible the new phase of finance capital. Taken together, these three phenomena are what I mean by 'globalization', a development which has potentially disastrous consequences for both people and planet.

Trade across continents goes back to ancient times. The Phoenicians, we know, sold their wares in Britain, and medieval Europe traded with China. The present form of world trade, however, has only been possible since the advent of air transport and, later, container ships. American companies, followed by European and Asian ones, found it to their advantage to set up production units in different parts of the world to take advantage of cheap labour and more amenable regulatory and tax environments. Consumer durables came to have their parts produced in different countries: the Ford Escort, for example, is produced in 15 different countries. The character of international trade changed, with a substantial proportion consisting of transfers between the departments of transnational corporations (TNCs).

The ability of these corporations to set their prices has had an impact on the value and stability of many national currencies. In turn, national currencies themselves entered into global trading, far exceeding the value of goods and services transacted. When TNCs made their shares available to citizens of other countries they became multinational corporations (MNCs), and share markets became global.

How to respond to these developments theologically? The author of Ephesians writes: 'Our struggle is not against flesh and blood, but against the rulers, against the authorities, against the powers of this dark world, and against the spiritual forces of evil in the heavenly realms' (6.12; the title of this chapter reflects the Authorized Version's rendering of this verse). This is the language the American and British governments have used about terrorists, but, I shall argue, it is used more appropriately of the structures of world trade, and especially of the MNCs, or, more precisely, of the spirituality, the worldview, behind them. The theologian Walter Wink has taught us that the language of 'the powers' describes the accumulated spiritual power, the 'personality', of nations, cultures, corporations or other powerful groupings. We are familiar with the idea of different cultures having a distinctive ethos, that which makes them unique. Exactly the same applies to political parties and to corporations. This ethos can be life-affirming, but it can also be disastrously dehumanizing – like that of fascism, for example. Such spiritual structures are, Wink reminds us, created, fallen and can be redeemed (Wink, 1984, 1986, 1992). I believe that this provides the overall framework for thinking about globalization. In this chapter I shall set out my reasons, arguing that globalization is a form of imperialism, that it carries with it a contemptible account of what it means to be human, that it destroys our sense of being at home in the world, and that it threatens the ecosystem. I shall then conclude by asking what, in this context, redemption might mean.

Globalization as imperialism

If the economic structures behind globalization are 'powers' in the New Testament sense, then we must regard them as 'created'. That is to say, they are not, as some of their advocates imagine, necessary and non-negotiable ways of running the economy. Of course, we need structures for trade. Human beings have traded since there was first surplus, and trade has immensely enriched human history, not just in terms of monetary wealth and improved technology but in terms of the exchange of knowledge and ideas as well. The key question, however, is what we do about imbalances of power. The classical economists lauded the advantages of trade in terms of the theory of 'comparative advantage', according to which all communities exchange what they produce best. To use Ricardo's famous example: Britain produces iron, Portugal port: both benefit from the exchange. Even this example was specious, because Britain and Portugal were hardly equal at the time. The colonialism that was already in full swing when Ricardo wrote meant that whole economies were constructed around the provision of food, or commodities like tea or coffee or bananas, from the periphery to 'the core'. As we saw in 2002 with regard to coffee, this could render whole areas of the world vulnerable to a devastating fall in prices, causing misery to millions of people.

Today global trade is marked by huge imbalances of power so that, in 1998, 3 billionaires earned more than all the less developed nations in the UN put together. Figures compiled by the UN Development Programme, and by the World Bank, tell us that of the world's 100 largest economies, 50 are TNCs, that the top 200 corporations account for more than a quarter of world trade, have bigger sales than all but the top ten countries, employ only 0.78 per cent of the world's workforce, and for the most part do not pay tax. Their primary objective is to make money; their primary responsibility is to their shareholders. Globally, however, less than 1 per cent of the world's population own any stocks and shares. This means that more than half of the world's biggest economies are designed to serve less than 1 per cent of the world's people.

Corporation enthusiasts believe they exist to serve humanity. They have even been described using the rhetoric of the Suffering Servant of Isaiah. Their own corporate propaganda, however, tells a different story. Calgene, the California biotech company famous for its attempt to get a genetically modified tomato on the table, sets out its corporate agenda thus:

> Our objective is to control production with our partners from the production of foundation seed to the sale of the oil to our customers. We want complete control. The seed margins don't begin to cover the cost of investments we've made in the technology. The way you capture value added is selling oil – value-added oil at a premium to customers, period. So we and our partners will maintain complete control of the process. (Kneen, 1993: 140)

Similarly, the Chairman of McDonald's said in 1994, 'Our goal is to totally dominate the quick service industry worldwide . . . I want McDonald's to be more than a leader. I want McDonald's to dominate' (Ritzer, 1996: 5). 'As huge as our world of Coca-Cola is today', says an executive of that company, 'it is just a tiny sliver of the world we can create' (Barber, 1995: 68).

In order for such corporations to succeed in their aim, every country must adopt the Western capitalist model. What happened in eastern Europe after the fall of communism is a good example. These countries were talked by foreign advisers or bullied by international banks into thinking that laissez-faire capitalist economics is a self-sufficient system. That this is not the case is shown by the cultural collapse that has followed, 'savage and repulsive forms of behaviour, the plunder of the nation's wealth' (Alexander Solzhenitsyn, cited in Barber, 1995: 238). Such forms of behaviour follow wherever profit is our creed, but the priority of profit is part of any corporate charter. Corporations do not exist 'for the common good' but for profit, for their shareholders. But this means that they are wedded to injustice, something the criminologist John Braithwaite has demonstrated over and over again (Braithwaite, 1984).

It is part and parcel of globalization that the great corporations have factories and offices throughout the world, but this does not mean that there is no geographical centre to present developments. On the contrary, since the end of the Second World War this centre has been the United States, home to the

International Monetary Fund (IMF) and the World Bank. The North American journalist Thomas Friedman lauds this fact, describing the United States as 'not just a country' but a spiritual value, a role model, a beacon for the whole world. It is 'the ultimate benign hegemon and reluctant enforcer' and needs to recognize that 'The hidden hand of the market will never work without a hidden fist . . . And the hidden fist that keeps the world safe for Silicon Valley's technologies to flourish is called the US Army, Air Force, Navy and Marine Corps' (Friedman, 2000: 464–75). The North American sociologists James Petras and Henry Veltmeyer understand this process as simple imperialism. While the idea of globalization implies the interdependence of nations, they argue, imperialism emphasizes the domination and exploitation of less developed countries and labouring classes by imperial states and MNCs. The notion of imperialism matches the reality of the situation far better than that of globalization (Petras and Veltmeyer, 2001: 29–30).

A report in the *Financial Times* provides a good example. The paper reported the settlement of a dispute between a New York hedge fund and the government of Peru which had been settled in favour of the former. Elliott Associates bought defaulted bank loans at half their face value and then insisted on reclaiming them at their full value. US courts awarded the fund $58 million – money transferred directly from the poor of Peru to the rich in New York. Jubilee 2000, an organization campaigning for debt relief, commented: 'These people are trading in human misery. Elliott Associates are picking over the bones of the Peruvian economy like a pack of vultures. It may be just business to them but to the children of Peru it is school books, medicines and clean water' (*Financial Times*, 25 October 2000). Elliott have also targeted Ecuador, Ivory Coast, Panama, Poland and Congo. This is the reality of globalization, the true nature of the global market.

The question of human ends

At the end of Matthew's Gospel Jesus sends the disciples into all the earth, commanding them to baptize people 'in the name of the Father and of the Son and of the Holy Spirit' (Matthew

28.19). Contrary to some Christian understandings, this is not the legitimation of Christian imperialism but is about sharing a particular account of what it means to be human, as revealed in the story of Christ. The early community described the account of life which they derived from Jesus as good news, 'gospel', because, they believed, living according to God's purposes was the only way to avoid violence and destruction. The Christian gospel commends a life lived in reconciliation rather than alienation, through forgiveness rather than retribution, through peace rather than violence. Jesus taught his disciples to pray for the coming of the Kingdom, the realization of this state of affairs. The new communities that came into being around this gospel saw themselves as seedbeds of a new humanity. They offered a radical alternative to 'business as usual' (Mark 10.43) – which in those days meant the Roman empire and its will to power.

Empires tend to the same goal – rule or domination – and they operate according to the same logic, which is violence. Philosophers and theologians, on the other hand, always begin with the fundamental question of what life is about. In some of the earliest and most important reflections on economics, Aristotle remarks that our wealth-getting, the means by which a society sustains itself, is directed to the good life, which he took to be a life of disciplined reflection in which all pleasures were taken in moderation. Wealth in itself, he was quite clear, could not possibly be that good. Learning from Aristotle, Christian thinkers consistently asked how the economy could serve the human good. Medieval economics aimed at fairness, a proper reward for labour for both the producer and the merchant. We can take issue with their notions of justice, but their insistence that economics be subordinated to moral aims remains vital. The emphasis changed in the eighteenth century when Adam Smith set out his account of the human good in terms of the wealth realized by trade. We need not be cynical about this. He saw the immense increase in productivity made possible by the division of labour and trade unhampered by restrictive legislation, and he believed that this would, more or less, work for the good of all. In some respects he was right, as we see if we look at the colossal achievements of capitalism since his time. Two problems, however, attend an uncritical acceptance of his argument. First, he presupposed a broad moral consensus, and a large and generous account of what it means to be human. Today, however, the acquisition and enjoyment of wealth have become an alternative account of human ends. Getting and spending have become the human project. Corporate capital, with its vast sums spent on advertising in order to stoke the fires of demand, has raised to the fore only one vision of the good life and pushed out all others (Korten, 1995: 150–1). This vision is dehumanizing in a literal sense.

Second, the claim that free trade works for the common good is highly contentious. In every society the gap between the rich and the poor has grown in the years since the neo-liberal gospel was first preached and put into effect. In the former Soviet empire, one commentator observes, globalization has caused greater reverses than those inflicted by the war with Hitler (Burbach *et al.*, 1996: 118). And it is preached with a truly evangelical fervour. Global trade and IMF nostrums, structural adjustment programmes, the acquisition of debt, will make life better, we are told day in day out by the economics journals, by the spokesmen of the Bretton Woods institutions, by the advertising of corporate capital. Eventually. For some.

The evangelical fervour of the neo-liberals means that there really is a contest between two gospels, and for this reason the German theologian Ulrich Duchrow has insisted for 25 years that the global economy is a confessional issue for the churches in the same way that fascism was. Most Christian commentators regard this as an exaggeration. In view of what present structures are doing to both people and planet I believe it is a rather cool realism. We are faced with the question both Elijah and the Deuteronomists put to their people: Whom do you serve?

The local and the global

The gospel is addressed to all creatures, but the Church is always at heart and essentially local. 'To all the saints in Christ Jesus who are in Philippi' – or Corinth, or Ephesus, or Rome, or wherever. The Church is local in order to be universal. In the global economy these priorities are reversed. Standardization and uniformity seem to be almost inevitable outcomes of a globalized economy dominated by international corporations geared to mass production and marketing in a culturally homogenized world. The year-round availability of imported foods dissolves the particularity of local cuisine, based on the food in season. What it means to be local changes. A few control and initiate 'flows' and 'movements', but the vast majority have no say in what happens. Old industries disappear and – if you are lucky – new ones take their place, but often on the other side of the globe. In a globalized world, says Zygmunt Bauman, localities lose their meaning-generating and meaning-negotiating capacity and are increasingly dependent on sense-giving and interpreting actions which they do not control (Bauman, 1998: 3). All that will be left of indigenous cultures, it has been suggested with some plausibility, will be museums for the tourists, for what we find in most 'developed' countries is a pastiche of cultural motifs and styles, underpinned by a universal scientific and technical discourse (Smith, 1990: 176).

Media like the BBC and CNN have a huge global reach, and what is broadcast, whether it is news or *Dallas*, conveys the message of the consumer culture with its emphasis on youth, fitness, beauty, romance and freedom (Bauman, 1998: 53). Similarly, in their advertising campaigns the great corporations sell not just their products but American prosperity and imagery and thus its very soul (Barber, 1995: 60). For Ziauddin Sardar the Disney film *Pocahontas* is an apt expression of neo-colonialism: everything now belongs to a world dominated by America, and America is the apogee of all human civilizations and experience, the only perspective through which history is meaningful (Sardar, 1998: 116).

It is fundamentally within this framework that George Ritzer understands McDonaldization, which, he argues, has increased homogenization both in the United States and throughout the world. Wherever fast food chains are found, arising in competition with American models, food is rationalized and compromised so that it is acceptable to the tastes of all diners (Ritzer, 1996: 136). To those postmodern theorists who argue that diversity is on the increase, Ritzer replies that McDonaldization is here for the foreseeable future and influencing society at an accelerating rate (Ritzer, 1996: 148). Many people point to the phenomenon of 'glocalism' and the claim of MNCs such as Coca-Cola that they are in fact multi-local. The question is, however, whether this is not an extremely weak and superficial form of 'localism', a patina of difference on one underlying reality.

Honouring creation

'The earth is the Lord's, and everything in it' (Psalm 24.1). This belief traditionally led to an understanding of creation as grace. Saying 'grace' before meals was a sign of reverence for life. This is again something that has changed as science and technology have extended their scope. In particular it is manifest in the attempt of the great agrochemical corporations to patent seeds and medicines. But to patent life is really to play God. As Canadian farmer and agricultural campaigner Brewster Kneen puts it:

> Genetic engineering is an expression of ingratitude and disrespect, if not contempt. It is a vehicle, in practice, of an attitude of domination and ownership, as expressed in the assumption that it is possible, reasonable, and morally acceptable to claim ownership over life. The claim that it is possible to own life, at least to the extent of being able to claim a patent on a life process or life form, is so outrageous socially and ethically as to be hardly worth debating. (Kneen, 1999: 29)

Corporate lawyers would, of course, beg to differ, having created thousands of such patents over the past 30 years.

In the North we are no longer 'citizens' but 'consumers'. Well-meaning campaigners even believe we can harness 'consumer power', which is to try and fight fire with fire. To consume is to devour, to destroy. The consumer society is devouring the earth – its fish, its forests, its fertile land, its water. These basic goods, the foundation of life, become scarcer year by year. Even clean, fresh, unpolluted air becomes scarcer.

The consumer society makes manifest the ultimate paradox of capitalism, its underlying nihilism. The whole global economy is predicated on growth. It has to grow to live: but the earth is finite. In 1992 Alan Thein Durning remarked: 'If we attempt to prolong the consumer society indefinitely, ecological forces will dismantle it savagely' (Durning, 1992: 107). World population has more than doubled since 1962, and increases by 80 million per annum. Already water and fish resources are at breaking-point. Land is required to feed the 80 million extra mouths each year, but the amount of fertile land available (one-third of the planet's surface) is actually shrinking, due to desertification, urbanization and mechanized agriculture. Global warming, caused by CO_2 emissions from our vastly increased industrial activity, could make much more of the planet infertile (including Britain) and drown great numbers of us. Resources are not infinite. The idea that we can go on growing, as the IMF insists, at 4.5 per cent per year, is a conceit bred by the tunnel vision of those who have reduced economics to profit-making, who have lost sight of its intimate connection to justice and the virtues.

These facts are a fundamental part of globalization and they make clear that the frenzied 'growth' bound up with it is a cynical and hollow grabbing of gain for the present with no regard for future generations. It is the squandering of the earth. This profound contempt for creation is manifest in the nihilism of governments like the British government, which spends £1.5 million per day on nuclear weapons – weapons that can do nothing but destroy. It is also evident in the growth of 'mind-less' vandalism, drug abuse, the search for new sensations to stimulate jaded appetites. These things are simply the nihilism of the global economy writ small.

Redemption in a globalized world

The powers, says Walter Wink, are created, fallen, but can be redeemed. What does redemption mean in a globalized world?

First, we have to abandon the TINA doctrine, which is a form of fatalism. TINA ('There is no alternative') is part of the gospel of corporate capital. This doctrine is false. TINA says that things have to be this way because that is human nature.

Scratch any *Economist* editorial, any book or article by any defender of the market, and you find Social Darwinism, the survival of the fittest. There is no alternative because human beings are selfish and it is folly to try and 'buck human nature'. It is this fundamental belief that Christianity challenges. The medieval theologians believed that economics is subordinate to justice because they believed that sin is met by grace, and grace overcomes sin. They therefore could not believe that economics is fate. On the contrary, they believed that economics can be regulated for the common good by law and not be a question of 'dog eat dog'. Of course we do not want to return to medieval economics, but we do want to insist on the priority of ethics over economics. The task is to find new forms of economic governance in the interest of the whole human community, present and to come. Nothing prevents this but political will.

Second, we need to accept limits. We cannot have our cake and eat it. We cannot both give priority to the market and ensure a healthy and safe world for our children and their heirs. This is something that steady state economists like Herman Daly have been urging for years (Daly and Cobb, 1988). The idolatry of growth has to be surrendered for a truly economic approach – that is to say, one which cares for the human household and its future. The 'laws of the market' cannot provide this: they are destroying us all.

Third, another concern of Daly's: the injustices bred by market economics are as unsustainable as the ecological results. In 1960 the richest 20 per cent of the world's population had 30 times as much as the poorest 20 per cent; by 1989 they had 59 times as much, and the ratio has gone on increasing since then. In such a situation the maintenance of social bonds becomes impossible. A new emphasis on social justice is essential if the globalizing process is to be redeemed.

How to do this? Again, let me suggest three points. 'Speak up for those who cannot speak for themselves,' we read in Proverbs, 'for the rights of all who are destitute. Speak up and judge fairly; defend the rights of the poor and needy' (Proverbs 31.8–9). The prophetic task, the Church has always said, devolves now to the body of Christ. Walter Wink understands this task as involving the unmasking of the powers which, in our world, are not just nations but corporations. The first step in their redemption is to unmask their claims to work for the common good, for the environment, and for the poor. This is not a simple business because they have billions to spend on persuading us that black is white, and that those who oppose them are off their trolleys. But, as the tens of thousands involved in the World Social Forum have demonstrated, the resources are there to do it in the selfless research and campaigning of Third- and even, sometimes, of First-World scientists. Economics is not fate. It can be changed.

Second, 1 Peter describes the Christian community as 'a kingdom of priests'. The Church is in principle an egalitarian, democratic institution. Reclaiming democracy is at the heart of economic, and not just political, recovery. If democracy is to survive, reforms must not only get corporations out of politics but also limit the power of big money to influence the voting behaviour of ordinary citizens (Korten, 1995: 310). Tax exemptions for corporate expenditures related to lobbying, public education, public charities or political organizations of any kind should be eliminated, with a view to ending the involvement of for-profit corporations in 'educating' the public on issues of policy or the public interest. And George Monbiot comments that if political participation could break the bars of totalitarian state communism, it can certainly force elected governments to hold corporations to account. Globalization must be matched with internationalism: campaigning, worldwide, for better means of government (Monbiot, 2000: 357).

Finally, the struggle is about different spiritualities. In the Book of Common Prayer there is a rubric that, if there is any bread left after the eucharist, it should be 'reverently consumed'. 'Reverent consumption' is consumption with respect for creation as gift. All of us are caught up in the spirituality of the principalities and powers. Celebrating the eucharist week by week, however, must be understood as a detox, the creation of a counter-culture. The powers absolutize what they call the economy. But we are part of what Wendell Berry calls 'the great economy', the whole ecological system, which theologically understood is gift, grace. We need to build and internalize a culture based on gratitude and reverence for life, not on grab and run. This is a spiritual matter, at the heart of the contest with the powers. Faith, Paul teaches us, is hope against hope. We should not underestimate the forces of destruction. Do we also underestimate the power of the God of life?

References

Barber, Benjamin (1995), *Jihad vs McWorld*. Ballantyne, New York.

Bauman, Zygmunt (1998), *Globalization: The Human Consequences*. Polity Press, Cambridge.

Braithwaite, John (1984), *Corporate Crime in the Pharmaceutical Industry*. Routledge, London.

Burbach, Ronaldo, Nunez, Orlando and Kargarlitsky, Boris (1996), *Globalization and Its Discontents*. Pluto, London.

Daly, Herman and Cobb, John (1988), *For the Common Good*. Green Print, London.

Durning, Alan (1992), *How Much is Enough?* Earthscan, London.

Friedman, Thomas (2000), *The Lexus and the Olive Tree*. HarperCollins, London.

Kneen, Brewster (1993), *From Land to Mouth*, 2nd edn. NC Press, Toronto.

Kneen, Brewster (1999), *Farmageddon*. New Society, Gabriola, Canada.

Korten, David (1995), *When Corporations Rule the World*. Kumarian, CT.

Monbiot, George (2000), *Captive State: The Corporate Takeover of Britain*. Macmillan, London.

Petras, James and Veltmeyer, Henry (2001), *Globalization Unmasked: Imperialism in the Twenty First Century*. Zed Books, London.

Ritzer, George (1996), *The McDonaldization of Society*, 2nd edn. Pine Forge, Thousand Oaks, CA.

Sardar, Ziauddin (1998), *Postmodernism and the Other*. Pluto, London.

Smith, Anthony (1990), 'Toward a Global Culture?', in M. Featherstone (ed.), *Global Culture*. Sage, London.

Wink, Walter (1984), *Naming the Powers*. Fortress Press, Minneapolis.

Wink, Walter (1986), *Unmasking the Powers*. Fortress Press, Minneapolis.

Wink, Walter (1992), *Engaging the Powers*. Fortress Press, Minneapolis.

Part III

8

Offering Resistance to Globalization: Insights from Luther

CYNTHIA MOE-LOBEDA

What is distinct about Christian spirituality is that its life-breath is the living Spirit of Jesus Christ. In this chapter I shall consider how the insights of Luther offer resources to sustain faithful resistance to neo-liberal globalization – resistance that has as its motivating, life-giving force the living Spirit of Jesus Christ. My concern is to probe the following question: How might faith in Jesus Christ – and indeed the faith of Jesus Christ – enable moral–spiritual power (a) to resist (that is, to unmask and counter) global economic arrangements that contradict the two Christian moral norms of 'justice-making, self-respecting, neighbour-love' and 'regenerative Earth–human relations', and (b) to forge economic alternatives more consistent with those norms?

For Luther, *communio* (communion), expressed in three inseparable forms – eucharist, solidarity, and the communing community – is a wellspring of subversive moral agency for resistance to whatever thwarts the gift of abundant life for all, and for forging alternatives. I explore that notion through constructive encounter with Luther and in particular with five interrelated theological gems running through his work. They are his eucharistic economic ethics, his theology of Christ indwelling creation, his call to certain practices, his refusal to minimize the pervasive presence of human sin and his insistence that in brokenness and defeat the saving God is present and draws forth power. This chapter restricts its focus, for reasons of space, to the first two, yet when taken together these five strains form a window into *communio* as source of moral spiritual power for resistance to neo-liberal economic globalization.

Eucharistic economic ethics

According to Luther, economic activity is, ontologically, an act in relationship to neighbour, and all relations with neighbour are normed by one thing: Christians are to serve their neighbour's well-being while also meeting their own needs and those of their household. Widely accepted economic practices that undermine the widespread good or the well-being of the poor should be denounced on theological grounds, defied in daily practice, and replaced with radical alternatives.[1] Luther is vehement and specific about this. For him, neighbour-love in economic life entails not only social welfare provision, but also denouncing economic exploitation and forging alternative economic norms and practices. Preachers, he declares, are to preach (that is, speak the living Word of God) against exploitative economic practices.

Luther's economic ethics and his eucharistic theology are inseparable. The fruit of the Eucharist, 'properly practised', is a *communio* of moral agency that attends to human needs and privileges the needs of the vulnerable. Economic practices flow from the Eucharist. Hear Luther speaking about the sacrament that we call 'communion' or Eucharist:[2]

> by means of this sacrament, all self-seeking love is rooted out and gives place to that which seeks the common good of all.

> When you have partaken of this sacrament . . . your heart must go out in love and learn that this is a sacrament of love. As love and support are given you, you in turn must render love and support to Christ in his needy ones.

> The sacrament has no blessing and significance unless love grows daily and so changes a person that he is made one with the others.

> In times past this sacrament was so properly used, and the

people were taught to understand this fellowship so well, that they even gathered food and material goods in the church, and . . . distributed among those who were in need . . . this has all disappeared, and now there remain only the many masses and the many who receive this sacrament without in the least understanding or practising what it signifies . . . They will not help the poor.

Economic life as a practice of neighbour-love, according to Luther, transgressed the emerging capitalist order of his day. Two norms and two rules derived from his treatise 'Trade and Usury' illustrate this. Our task is to hear them in the light of neo-liberal globalization. The two norms are as follows:

1. Because selling is an act towards neighbour, its goal should be not profit but rather serving the needs of the other and making 'an adequate living' for oneself and one's household.[3]
2. Economic activity should be subject to political constraints. Luther writes: 'Selling ought not to be an act that is entirely within your own power and discretion, without law or limit.' Civil authorities should establish 'rules and regulations', including 'ceilings' on prices.[4]

According to these norms designed to protect the poor, Christians are to follow firm rules in economic life. They include:

- Do not buy a commodity when cheap and then sell when the price goes up.
- Do not sell at a price as high as the market will bear.[5]

Economic structures and practices denounced by Luther for the sake of neighbour-love also undergird economic globalization in its dominant form today. So close is the coherence that, were Luther's norms to be adopted as guiding principles for contemporary life, they would subvert the prevailing paradigm of economic globalization. Luther's economic norms challenge specific dynamics inherent in that paradigm, including

(1) elevating 'profit', rather than 'an adequate living', as the goal of economic life; (2) pricing commodities as high as the market will bear, where so doing undermines the well-being of the poor; and (3) severing economic activity from political constraints (by means of deregulation). Luther's impassioned economic ethics denounced unregulated market activity that enabled a few to make a profit at the expense of the common good or the well-being of the poor.[6] Many of his words speak so directly to the global economy today that they mirror the claims of its critics. I was reading Luther in Seattle during the summit of the World Trade Organization in 1999 in that city. I found to my surprise that the words of Luther and of the protestors outside the summit venue were, at times, the same! I tested my perceptions out in a lecture I gave soon afterwards, reading out quotes and asking students to indicate whether the words were Luther's or the protesters'. They could not tell!

My point is *not* to advocate a direct and uncritical application of Luther's economic analysis or norms to the contemporary situation. Given his inflammatory denunciations of Jews, peasants and Anabaptists, never are his social analyses or ethics to be adopted uncritically as normative. Doing so would lack intellectual and moral integrity. I also do not intend to imply that Luther was a 'progressive' early anti-capitalist. That implication would be false, failing to acknowledge that his condemnation of emerging capitalism and his crafting of alternative economic norms and practices were not rooted in a bent towards progressive social change (which was not within his conceptual world). Luther's critique was rooted, social-theoretically, in his 'conservative' defence of feudal social arrangements and prohibitions on interest.

Rather, the salient points are these: Luther's economic ethics had subversive implications in his context – a context which bears uncanny resemblances to that of economic globalization today. The subversive nature of Luther's economic norms, and the moral power for heeding them, derive from their theological foundation: neighbour-love, manifest in economic life, and *empowered by Christ's indwelling presence*. That point is crucial. Luther's economic ethic depends upon his claim that God as the love of Christ actually comes to live within and among the

community of believers. That indwelling Christ-presence *is* the
power to love, and love is manifest in – though not only in –
economic life.

Christ indwelling

To that indwelling presence we now turn. According to Luther,
God indwells earthlings who trust him, and in fact and in
mystery God 'must be essentially present in all places even in
the tiniest leaf'.[7] God is 'present in every single creature in its
innermost and outermost being'.[8] The finite bears the infinite.
The God of unbounded love has made habitation in the
community gathered and sent forth by bread and wine, and in
the creatures and elements of this good Earth.

What are the implications of this for moral–spiritual power?
A key one is that Christ as unmerited gift dwells within and
among communities of believers and gradually transforms them
towards a manner of life that actively loves neighbour by serving
their well-being and receives the same in return. Luther writes:
'[T]his is . . . one of the exceedingly great promises granted to
us . . . that we should even have the Lord Himself dwelling
completely in us.'[9] 'One in whom God dwells makes daily
progress in good works, and is useful to God and to others.'[10]
'Christians are indeed made the habitation of God, and in them
God speaks, and rules, and works';[11] they are 'changed into one
another and are made into a community by love'.[12] Identity
understood as the 'habitation' of Christ establishes the purpose
of human activity, which is this: to live not for oneself alone but
for all people.[13] For Luther, then, the centrepiece of Christian
moral spiritual agency is the crucified and living Christ
dwelling in and gradually transforming the community of
believers, the form of Jesus Christ taking form in and among
those of faith. Christians as objects of Christ's love become
subjects of that love. Faith is both faith *in* Christ and the faith
of Christ. The moral life is therefore both gift and imperative, a
mystical as well as physical reality, ontologically communal
while also individual, a necessary outflow of the sacraments.[14]

Evangelical resistance to hegemonic authority, where that
resistance is life-threatening, requires courage. For Luther, the

most powerful courage known to humankind is generated by the Spirit and Christ living in the faithful. The Spirit may bring into its human abode 'true courage – boldness of heart'. 'The Hebrew word for spirit', Luther preaches, 'might well be rendered "bold, undaunted courage".'[15] That 'bold, dauntless courage . . . will not be terrified by poverty, shame, sin, the devil, or death, but is confident that nothing can harm us and we will never be in need'.[16] This empowering courage is, according to Luther, greater than any human force on Earth.

Let us be clear: for Luther, becoming the dwelling-place of Christ and agent of his love *cannot* be earned by human effort, and cannot, in any way, earn salvation. Quite the opposite. Christ's indwelling and transforming presence is pure unearned gift, and is a *consequence* of salvation by God's grace alone. The significance is moral and anthropological, not soteriological.

Note, too, Luther's insistence that the change towards neighbour-love is never fully completed within a lifetime. 'Christians are indeed called and made the habitation of God, and in them God speaks, and rules, and works. But the work is not yet complete; it is an edifice on which God yet works daily and makes arrangements.'[17]

Luther's theology of God indwelling creation hints at another source of moral power. Luther insisted, as already noted, that God's indwelling presence is given not only to human beings, but to all parts of creation, 'even in the tiniest leaf'. God is present 'in every single creature in its innermost and outermost being'.[18] God as boundless, justice-seeking love coursing through creation implies that all creatures and elements may offer creative, saving, sustaining power towards creation's flourishing. To think theologically about the moral agency that flows from God inhabiting all of created reality is to struggle for and with a concept that barely exists in Western Protestant ethics. Luther's indwelling God opens that door theologically.

Considered in the context of neo-liberal economic globalization, the claim that the gracious mystery of God resides in all matter and there works towards the flourishing of creation provokes countless questions. How may this indwelling God-power free us as people of economic privilege *from* immobilization in the face of economic forces and *for* faithful resistance on behalf of the community of the Earth and its cultures? And, if the Earth's life-giving and life-saving capacities are being destroyed by our daily practices, as dictated by the workings of the global economy, are those ways of life – our ways of life – not crucifying Christ?

Luther offers profound theological resources stemming from a eucharistic notion of Christ loving within the *communio*, turning earthlings into subversive lovers on behalf of the common good. This is important moral wisdom, especially for Lutheran communions and their friends in faith. However, it must be admitted that we do not need Luther to arrive here. Some Orthodox and Anglican theologies, recent cosmic Christologies, eco-theologies, and some feminist relational theologies also emphasize God's indwelling of all creation and his working through all creatures and elements to save, heal, liberate the entire household of life.

So what is the provocative pull of Luther? What is the insistent tweak that says 'plumb the depths here, because there is more and the world is hungering for it'? Three things. All nurture hope. They are the third, fourth and fifth 'theological gems' mentioned above. I simply note them.

Practices, pervasive presence of sin, and the cross

Luther identifies concrete and ancient practices through which the living Christ is proclaimed and received, becomes incarnate in the community of believers and there calls forth moral power to swim upstream against powerful social forces. These practices include the Eucharist, prayer, and being with and for those who suffer (in other words, solidarity). In fact, for Luther, communion as Eucharist and communion as solidarity go hand in hand. To reconsider seriously these practices, and to do so in line with Luther's theo-ethical method, is to uncover vital insights into the roots of subversive moral spiritual power for resisting neo-liberal globalization and forging more life-saving alternatives.

Luther's sense of profound moral agency flowing from the indwelling Christ is accompanied by his equally strong insistence on the pervasive presence of sin, the humanly insurmountable reality that human beings are turned in on themselves, or literally 'self curved in on self' (*se encurvatus en se*). This is surely a strikingly descriptive and deeply truthful account of reality in the globalizing economy. According to Luther, it is not possible for us to do the moral good as fully as we try to do it. Luther's paradoxical moral anthropology speaks directly to the heart of life for economically privileged people. Collectively, we are selves curved in on ourselves. We may long to live according to justice-making, self-honouring love for the earth and for neighbour. But in the United States at least, we have become so addicted to our economic ways that we close our eyes to the death and destruction required to sustain them. We do not see clearly the vision of Mozambique's Bishop Bernardino Mandlate, that our economic privilege is bought with 'the blood of African children'. Needing expanding markets, short-term financial gains, fossil fuels and inexpensive goods, we will lie, kill and beef up brutal regimes: the Taliban and Osama Bin Laden in their war against Russia; Saddam Hussein in his war against Iran while he was gassing the Kurds; Marcos; Somoza – all products, to an extent, of our need to access and control resources, markets and, more recently, labour. The drive to dominate and exploit is a drive of 'self curved in on self', the polar opposite of serving the needs of others and particularly those who suffer.

Luther's insistence, then, that we are 'selves curved in on self' serves as a dialectical partner to his claim that the indwelling Christ renders profound moral agency. This dialectic is crucial to evangelical resistance for people of economic privilege. For them, a principal task of Christian spiritual resistance is to see two realities in one gaze. One is the socio-ecological realities in which we live, including our implication in economic violence. From seeing these, we tend to run with body, heart and clever mental manipulations. That running – in the forms of avoidance, denial and retreat into private morality – enables economic brutality to continue. But 'critical seeing' is painful and threatening. It burns people up, unless it is wed to seeing, in the same gaze, a second reality. This is the life-giving, life-saving, life-sustaining power of God coursing through the *communio* and through all of creation, a God whose love for this world cannot be thwarted by any force on heaven or earth.

Finally, Luther's paradoxical moral anthropology lives within a theological claim that *where God seems hidden, there God is*. As Larry Rasmussen has said, 'the only power that can truly heal creation is instinctively drawn to the broken and flawed places in life, there is most fully known, and precisely there draws forth power'.[19] God is drawn into the brokenness of this world – including the bondage of some to ways of life that brutalize – and there becomes life-saving power incarnate. Luther's theology of the cross, held together with God's indwelling and empowering of the *communio* of all creation, renders the promise without which to open one's eyes to the 'data of despair' might be to drown in it. That Christ fills all things, and is present particularly in sites of suffering, enables us to acknowledge soul-searing economic brutalities that must be faced if we are to resist neo-liberal economic globalization, and convert to economic ways that enable just and sustainable communities and Earth community for generations to come.

We have entered the mystery that God's love in Christ is flowing and pouring into the *communio* gathered and sent forth by bread and wine for justice-making, self-honouring neighbour-love in all aspects of life. That claim – explored through a wedding of Luther's eucharistic economic ethics, his theology of Christ indwelling creation, his call to certain practices, his refusal to minimize the pervasiveness of human sin and his insistence that in brokenness and defeat the saving God is present and draws forth power – points a way towards spiritual power for resistance to global economic arrangements that breed injustice and suffering. According to Luther, in the *communio* the incarnate God is embodied as justice-making, self-honouring neighbour-love made manifest in economic life. In the context of neo-liberal globalization, such neighbour-love is faithfully subversive.

Notes

1. Luther, 'Trade and Usury', in *Luther's Works*, vol. 45, ed. Walther I. Brandt (Muhlenberg Press, Philadelphia, 1962), pp. 44–308.
2. The statements that follow are from Luther, 'The Blessed

Sacrament of the Holy and True Body and Blood of Christ, and the Brotherhoods', in *Martin Luther's Basic Theological Writings*, ed. Timothy Lull (Fortress Press, Minneapolis, 1989), pp. 260, 247, 251 and 250 respectively.

3. Luther, 'Trade and Usury', p. 250.
4. Luther, 'Trade and Usury', pp. 249–50.
5. Luther, 'Trade and Usury', p. 261; see also pp. 247–51.
6. Luther, 'The Large Catechism', in *The Book of Concord*, ed. Theodore G. Tappert (Fortress Press, Philadelphia, 1959), p. 397. In 'The Large Catechism', see also his comments on the first, fifth, sixth, seventh and ninth/tenth commandments.
7. Luther, 'That These Words of Christ, "This is My Body", etc. Still Stand Firm Against the Fanatics', in *Luther's Works*, vol. 37, ed. Helmut T. Lehmann (Muhlenberg Press, Philadelphia, 1962), p. 57.
8. Luther, 'That These Words', p. 58.
9. Luther, 'Third Sermon on Pentecost Sunday', in *Sermons of Martin Luther*, ed. John Lenker, 8 vols (Baker, Grand Rapids, MI, 1983), 3.316–17.
10. Luther, 'Third Sermon', in *Sermons*, 3.317.
11. Luther, 'Third Sermon', in *Sermons*, 3.321.
12. Luther, 'The Blessed Sacrament', p. 251.
13. Luther, 'Freedom of a Christian', in *Martin Luther's Basic Theological Writings*, p. 616.
14. Cynthia Moe-Lobeda, *Healing a Broken World: Globalization and God* (Fortress Press, Minneapolis, 2002), p. 74.
15. Luther, in *Sermons*, 8.275.
16. Luther, in *Sermons*, 8.275–6.
17. Luther, 'Third Sermon', in *Sermons*, 3.321.
18. Luther, 'That These Words', p. 58.
19. A statement made in a classroom lecture by Larry Rasmussen at Union Theological Seminary.

9

Campaigning against Injustice and the Appeal to Self-Interest

MICHAEL TAYLOR

The global economy is not the whole of globalization, but it is a very large part of it. It is all-embracing, aided and abetted by information technology, and characterized by privatization, free markets, open borders and a striking preoccupation with making money. There are two diametrically opposed opinions about it. Some believe it is the best hope of the poor, others that it does the poor no good at all. I shall make four points about this fundamental divergence of views.

United about injustice

First, there is no necessary disagreement between the two camps about the unacceptability of poverty, or gross inequality, or marginalization. You can believe in the global economy, as many of the people I know and work with passionately do, or you can dismiss the global economy along with the anti-globalization campaigners, but you can still join hands and cry together against injustice. You can disagree about the cause and you can disagree about the cure but you can still agree about injustice. You can still agree that it exists and is contrary to everything we have learned as Christian people from the Old Testament law and prophets, from Jesus himself, and from the great crowd of witnesses who have sought after God's Kingdom and his righteousness. And you can still be committed as a Christian and as a human being to getting rid of it. For or against the economic system, people on both sides can be and are against injustice.

Two of the most obvious examples of that injustice in the world today are about work and visas. When it comes to work, rich and poor can both be work-shy and lazy, and prefer to sit in the sun or take whatever handouts they can get. But most people, rich or poor alike, are hard-working. They have a sense of pride and a desire to make their own way and earn their keep and look after themselves and their families. But hard work does not bring comparable, let alone equal, rewards. The rich can work hard; the poor often work harder, and a poor woman works even harder than poor men: fetching and carrying water, cooking and washing, carrying and caring for children, cleaning the house, looking after domestic animals, going to the fields, and all for little or nothing. Equally, hard work over long hours does not reap equitable returns.

Then there are the visas. If a wealthy financier wishes to move his money from one country or continent to another, not to invest in its future and take the rough with the smooth along with its people but to speculate and make more money, he needs no visa, or passport, or entry permit that allows his money to travel. His money can move at will – often at the flick of a switch – to make more money, or avoid the taxes on the money he has already. But what about a poor man or woman with only the work of their hands and their skills to travel with, who wish to go from one country to another to try and make a better living and take care of their families? For them the border-crossing by boat, by train, by night, by lorry, by whatever, is far more difficult, even impossible, with visas and passports and permits and identity cards all required as well as excuses, if they are not to be turned back as bogus asylum seekers or illegal immigrants. Money can travel and prosper. Poor people cannot.

Being constructive

The second point is that there is no necessary difference in the morality of those who believe the global economy is good for the poor and those who believe it does them no good at all. If we join the anti-globalization campaigners we cannot necessarily claim the moral high ground; and it would be dishonest and unfair to suggest that members of the World Bank staff, for example, are indifferent to the poor and less committed than those who demonstrate against their policies and practices. Both sides can have moral integrity. Both sides can abhor poverty and wish to put an end to it. Where they disagree is about how to do it.

Demonizing the opposition can miss the point and let us off the hook. The most important argument may not be a moral argument but a technical one – not about who is better but about how best to get things done. So where lies our responsibility as Christian people? If we really want to love our neighbour and actually do our neighbour a bit of good, the biggest challenge is not to have a hot head but a cool head and a clear one. We are against injustice and poverty; but if we believe the present economic system will never put matters right, then it is our Christian vocation to find a better one. We must stand up and be counted not just for what we are against but for what we are for. The biblical tradition says 'No' to injustice but it says 'Yes' to a new creation. It calls us to break down what should not stand, but even more urgently it calls us to be creative and constructive and to build new worlds.

In general, we have been better at saying 'No' or keeping quiet than proposing alternatives. Or we are sidetracked into the more comfortable territories of debate – about spirituality, for example, or more holistic approaches to life, or neglected cultural issues. These are important, but they can never supplant the fundamental importance of finding a way to make the world's economy work so that everyone can have enough food, education, shelter and healthcare and a decent standard of living. Economics are not everything – of course they are not. But very little else is going to count if the basic economic necessities of life are not taken care of.

So if we do not like this global economy, we are required as Christians to campaign for what we do like. We are not just 'breakers'. We are called to be 'makers'. That seems to me to have at least three practical implications.

First, as Christians we should recognize the importance of research into economic issues and alternatives and be ready to honour and support it. The Christian Aids, CAFODs,

Tearfunds and Jubilee Campaigns of this world should not have to apologize for one minute when they build up and resource and coordinate think-tanks and research departments with our money, and get their minds to work on restructuring the global economy so that it favours the poor; on trading regulations that give everyone a chance to sell and buy in the marketplace; on global taxation systems that might help to redistribute wealth; on internalized economies that make maximum use of a community's own resources so that they are not completely dependent on an often hostile outside world; or on better ways to handle debt and the so-called economic basket cases; or on economic systems that respect and reward everybody's contributions. As Christians we must be economically as well as theologically literate. We must campaign for what will work; and we should impress on a rising generation that if they feel called by Christ to put first his Kingdom then in this day and age they should seriously consider a vocation to development economics.

The second practical implication is that we should insist that any research into economic alternatives should be carried out in a thoroughly participatory way. Theoretical economists sitting in universities and banks and agencies and research units have a big part to play, but they cannot deliver by themselves. Committed and clever people from our own Northern culture, brought up in a Western rationalist tradition, have a part to play, but they cannot deliver by themselves either. The search for alternatives must involve people on the ground, especially poor people, with their untidy experience and the kind of knowledge that can only be gained from patience and practice. Like the rest of us they do not know everything, but they are just as wise as we are, and we cannot be wise without them.

There is a third practical implication. The general run of we ordinary, everyday Christians are not competent to go and argue the toss with Treasury officials, transnational corporations (TNCs), or the staff of the World Bank, the International Monetary Fund (IMF) or the World Trade Organization (WTO). We must nevertheless take our cue from those who are and back them up with our campaigning power on the streets on May Day, with our consumer power in the superstores, with our investment decisions, with our democratic power, with the power of our faith and of our prayers – powers which we still fail to even begin to exploit for the sake of the poor, or honour as authentic forms of Christian discipleship.

The line of argument in this chapter so far has been that a large part of what we are about when we face up to the so-called opposition is not a moral argument with them but a technical argument about what will work better for the poorest of the poor than the present global economic system. If we don't like what we've got we are called as Christians to positively seek out, advocate and build a new economic order.

Divided by self-interest

The third point has to do with the question why the division of opinion that I drew attention to at the beginning of this chapter occurs. Why do these diametrically opposite views arise: one believing that the global economy is the only hope for the poor, the other believing it is no good for the poor at all? Of course there are lots of reasons. We come at these things from different angles. We have different histories and backgrounds and experiences. We make different assumptions which tend to colour the evidence. One person's knowledge and experience is different from another's and all of our views are partial because none of us can ever know it all.

But over and above all this there is one highly significant reason why we are attracted to one position rather than another. It is hugely dependent on where our self-interests lie, or where we think they lie. If we think a policy will benefit us – however little it may benefit anyone else – we tend to be in favour of it. If we think a policy will be to our disadvantage – even if it benefits other people – we are more than likely to be against it, though we usually try to find high-sounding and objective reasons for doing so rather than selfish ones.

Opinions divide according to self-interest. Here again there is no intrinsic difference between the two sides of the economic argument or between rich and poor. Those who take one view cannot claim the selfless high ground over those who take the opposite view. Self-interest is always busy at work on all sides.

Take theology as a quite different example from the economy. It can be argued that the Western Church – our Church – has been dominated for much of its history by a theology that focuses on our sinful disobedience, our broken relationship with God, the punishment we deserve under God's law, and the forgiveness and reconciliation made possible by the sacrifice of Christ if only we will repent and put our faith and trust in him. It is a theology that tends to focus on us as individuals and on our private lives and innermost relations with God. It is a very personal theology. It applies to everyone, rich and poor alike, since all are sinners. It prioritizes no-one, and it is all too easy to accept its invitation and turn to Christ and find hope and comfort without any change in the social order whatsoever. It is a theology that is attractive to powerful people whose vested interest is in keeping the social order as it is because it benefits them. And the Western Church has generally been the church of powerful people, who have tended to rule their world.

The theology that has characterized some of the churches of the South in recent years is quite different. We call it 'liberation theology'. It does not offer personal salvation through Christ without any social change but a highly political social revolution where everything changes and freedom in Christ is not so much freedom from guilt and sin but freedom from oppression and injustice. It prioritizes the poor and says they must come first. It is a theology that is attractive to powerless people and communities whose vested interest is in getting rid of a social order which does them no favours and replacing it with one where they might have a chance to spread their wings and prosper.

One of these theologies may well be right and the other wrong. Both may contain a measure of the truth. That is not the point. The point is that what divides us in favour of one or the other is where our self-interest lies: for the rich it lies in the status quo, for the poor, in radical change.

The same is true when we opt not for a theology but for an economic system. There is an important technical argument to be had about what will work; and there is a highly significant vested-interest argument to be had about what works for me and for us – whether we can prosper in the economic order as it is or whether we only see ourselves as losers unless it is radically changed.

All of us, rich and poor, relatively rich and relatively poor, have our own self-interests and tend to act on them. That is not the difference between us. The real difference is that we do not all have the same opportunity to act on them. Some are in a far stronger position to pursue their self-interests than others: the US is in a stronger position than Iraq; Israel is in a stronger position than the Palestinians; TNCs are in a stronger position than coffee growers in Ethiopia; the G8 is in a stronger position than HIPCs (heavily indebted poor countries); the World Bank and the IMF are in a stronger position than many a poor nation-state; the middle classes are in a stronger position than those who stand in the benefits queue; citizens of democracies like ours are in a stronger position than people in countries where civil society can hardly afford to organize at all; and citizens of industrial countries are in a stronger position than immigrants from a poor one. The crucial issue when push comes to shove is the issue of power.

Campaigning strategies

So my fourth and final point is about how we should be campaigning for an improved economic order in the corridors of power and out on the streets.

If the issue is fundamentally a matter of power, first, we do not want to campaign merely for a reversal of power – a kind of Magnificat upside-down world where the mighty are removed from their thrones and the poor get their chance to sit on them for a change. It might be only fair to give the poor a turn but, in the long run, they would start behaving like their predecessors. No, the campaigning strategy is not to reverse power but to share power: so that everyone has a better chance of pursuing their own self-interest and no-one is left with so much power to push everyone else around that their self-interest dominates.

This is a strategy that digs deep into our Christian understanding of human nature. On the one hand we all reflect the image of God. We are all capable of being generous and creative

– and of imaginatively making the new economic worlds we discussed earlier. On the other hand, our nature is profoundly insecure. We tend to protect ourselves and our self-interest, and we use whatever power we have to do so. So according to Christian realism power has to be shared: your power has to check mine and mine has to check yours and someone else's has to check both if we are to prevent the worst of injustice, including economic injustice.

That is why, for example, we raise the alarm if Malawi has a weak voice at the WTO while the US or the UK has a loud one which can drown out all the rest. That is why we raise the alarm if TNCs and their money are able to travel the world unfettered while nation-states struggle to control their own financial affairs and care for their people. That is why we raise the alarm if democracy is so weak and unreal that corrupt dictators can have their way and steal or misuse the limited resources of their countries. That is why we raise the alarm if deals are done about loans for development, debt repayment or poverty reduction plans without local people and their organized networks (which we call 'civil society') having a seat at the table and a say in what is going on. That is why we raise the alarm when poor people and badly paid workers and people on even less than a minimum wage are marginalized and divided and organizationally weakened so that those who exploit them can trample on their rights and dignities as human beings.

But recognizing the significant role played by self-interest leads to a second campaigning strategy. Madeleine Bunting has written that 'guilt is a crucial part of the Western moral tradition . . . guilt is what is most likely to prompt you to change'.[1] I do not altogether agree with her. Guilt is certainly a crucial part of the Western moral tradition, as I have just indicated in my rather crude account of the general tone of Western theology. But we handle our guilt rather well so that we learn to live with it in a state of forgiving acceptance; and it changes nothing. I doubt that 'guilt' is most likely to prompt us to change. It could be, however, that 'fear' will change us. Above all, it will be a shift in our perceptions of where our real self-interest lies that is most likely to prompt us to change.

The US oil industry, for example, will go on fighting to protect its supplies across the world or securing its supplies within its own safer Northern American borders, independent of the hazards and misfortunes of the rest of the world. It will go on allowing the car industry and its opportunities for jobs and profits to grow. This will continue until or unless the growing environmental catastrophe caused by conflict, and the destruction of the land, and the pollution of the air – choking and flooding human life into abject misery through storm and tempest and the rising of the waters – is brought home to us. Only then will a quite proper and well-founded fear alter our perceptions of where our real self-interest lies.

Similarly, the rich, including ourselves, will go on making money as fast as we can, apparently at the expense of the majority rather than for everybody's benefit. This will continue until or unless the explosive potential of the situation we are creating is brought home to us, with its deep divides and growing resentments. When finally we are instilled with a quite proper and well-founded fear of a global conflict that will not just terrify but consume us all, our perceptions as to where our real self-interests lie will be radically changed.

So our strategy must be first to frighten people to death with the consequences of what they are doing and then, second, to persuade them that their self-interest lies elsewhere, in a more attractive alternative to a global rat-race. Such an alternative would take a more rounded, cooperative and tolerant approach to human life on earth in which no-one would be the loser, not even ourselves, and all should have prizes because all would have won their share in the common good.

In the Christian tradition from which I come, many a preacher of a past generation used that first campaigning tactic to win converts, and often to good effect. He (and it was always he) would make it absolutely clear in a forceful way that his congregation were sinners, up to no good, doing what was evil in God's sight, condemned as guilty and heading for the rich punishment they deserved – and it was all on a rather personal and individual and private level. We are called to make it absolutely clear to even bigger 'secular' congregations that we are up to no good and largely responsible for it and heading for the dire consequences of what we are doing – a wasteland instead of a homeland – but all on a much more social and community and public level.

However, the old-fashioned preacher was never out to frighten people to death so much as to frighten them into life, and we must do the same. The old-fashioned preacher knew there was more to it than bad news. He had good news to preach as well. In our day, that cannot mean frantically preaching a gospel calculated merely to benefit the Church and recruit new members into its ranks. It certainly cannot be the prosperity gospel which gains ground among both rich and poor. It has to be the good news that there is a common good or a common self-interest that can include us all, and that while we can never realize it completely, as if the Kingdom of God could come on earth, we can set our eyes on it and move nearer to it with every step we take rather than move further away.

We are partly back to our calling to say what we are 'for', not just what we are against, and to make sure we are well informed when we say it. But we are also back to matters of faith. If we are to preach what we believe, surely Christians believe that a socio-economic order, just like a local community order or a family order, will work in our self-interest and will lead to human flourishing when (in contrast to our present global economic order) it is suffused and shaped by solidarity, generosity, self-giving, inclusiveness, tolerance, respect and sharing. This is the gospel! This is the good news! This is the attractiveness of the good that we should be preaching with all the evangelical fervour and persistence and appetite for conversion we can muster and that we sometimes devote to gospels that are far less true or important. If we are serious about change we have to persuade our generation that its own self-interest is other than it thinks.

Conclusion

In conclusion, as we go out as Christians to campaign on the streets and elsewhere (and campaign we must, not only 'on behalf of' the poor and 'for' the poor, but 'with' the poor), we should be clear on the following six points and the way they need to go together. First, that God says an absolute 'No' to injustice and poverty. Second, that there are no grounds for demonizing the opposition and arrogating to ourselves the moral high ground: as people we are as bad and as good as each other. Third, that we must say what we are 'for' and not just what we are against. If we judge that the present order will not do we must lobby and campaign for the best alternative we know of, well researched in practice and in theory and drawing on the wisdom of us all. Fourth, we must take full account of the darker side of human nature which will always use power selfishly if it gets the chance, and campaign for measures that distribute power and restrain it. A mere wish-list of ideals will help no-one. Fifth, we should frighten people with the consequences of what we are doing as we turn God's earth into a conflictual wasteland, which is in nobody's interest at all. Sixth, we should be evangelists for the more attractive possibility we believe in, reflected as it is in the quirky parables of the Bible, where prodigals come home, outsiders become insiders, people do not live by bread alone, the poor become rich, even late-comers get a decent wage, threatening enemies become attractive objects of love, and limited supplies of bread and fish suddenly become more than enough for all.

Note

1. *The Guardian*, 11 February 2002.

10

Changing the Wind:
The Role of Prophetic Witness and Faith-Based Initiatives in Tackling Inequality

JIM WALLIS

As an American offering a perspective on global poverty and inequality, I want to make a disclaimer. This is not the official White House version, but a perspective from the viewpoint of faith. I believe that the times cry out for new faith-based initiatives. These are likely to be far more significant than the US and UK governments imagine when they encourage such initiatives. The encouragement comes because of the work people of faith are doing on the ground. I can point to neighbourhoods all over the US where some of the best work being done on youth violence, job training, healthcare and low-income housing proceeds from the basis of faith. But while political leaders invite our social service provision, they don't often invite our prophetic witness. So I would suggest today that faith communities have to offer their prophetic witness uninvited.

When I think of faith-based initiatives, I don't think immediately of the White House. I think of the inmates at Sing Sing Prison in upstate New York, who asked if I would come and speak. I wrote back and said: 'Sure, when would you like me to come?' They replied: 'Well, we're free most nights – we're kind of a captive audience here.' So I went. The prison officials were wonderful; they gave us a room way down in the bowels of the prison and left us alone for about five hours. I talked with 75 guys for most of the evening. I'll never forget what one of those young inmates said to me. 'At Sing Sing, we are all from about five neighbourhoods in New York City. It's like a train,' he said, 'you get on that train when you're nine or ten years old in my neighbourhood and that train ends up here.'

That young man was converted inside the prison walls. So he said: 'When I get out, I want to go back and stop that train.' When you're in prison, you're just about at the bottom of the bottom. And when those at the bottom of the bottom have a faith-based initiative, it can stop urban trains full of young kids destined for prison.

Changing the wind

My topic in this chapter is change. It's about removing whole systems of economic domination. And it's about undertaking this project as a faith-based initiative. I was recently at a rally on the famous Mall in Washington. Two thousand people on low wages were there to lobby their Members of Congress and I was there to speak to them. We had important legislation coming up that would have a dramatic impact on poor families. So I said to them: 'You're here to lobby your Members of Congress. Let me tell you how to recognize a Senator or a Congressperson. Here's how you know – they're the ones who are always licking their fingers and putting them in the air to see which way the wind is blowing.' We often make the mistake of thinking you can replace one wet-fingered politician with another and change things. When nothing changes, we get disappointed, and we forget what the great leaders of social movements have always understood: that you change a nation by changing the wind. If you do that, it's amazing how quickly political leaders begin to shift their positions. If we're going to face our historical moment clearly – with eyes wide open and no illusions – then we're going to have to change the wind about fundamental issues like poverty. Why do almost half the world's people live on less than $2 per day and over one billion live on less than $1 per day? Because the wind has been blowing in the wrong direction. Lobbying for small incremental changes is not enough. We have to change the whole perception of things.

Martin Luther King, a good Baptist preacher, was my mentor. He taught me about changing the wind. He did that for the US on the issue of race – he changed the way we thought, he changed our moral sensibilities. That's what our times cry out for. And I believe there are signs that the wind is changing.

The unabridged Bible

Recently I went back to preach at my old seminary, Trinity Evangelical Divinity School. It's very evangelical and conservative. When I left there 30 years ago they were happy to see me go, so I was a bit apprehensive. In my sermon I recalled that as a young seminarian, in a place that revered the Bible, a group of us did a Bible study on poverty. We found every biblical text that said something about the poor and discovered it amounted to a great wide stream – the second most prominent theme in the Old Testament. The first was idolatry, and the two were closely connected.

In the New Testament, we found that one in every 16 verses is about the poor. In the synoptic Gospels it was one in every ten verses; in the Gospel of Luke, one in every seven verses. One of my fellow students thought he'd try something. He took an old Bible and a pair of scissors, and he began to cut out of the Bible every single text about the poor – he just snipped it right out. He got to Amos: 'Let justice roll on like a river, righteousness like a never-failing stream!' (Amos 5.24). He cut it out. Isaiah: 'Is not this the kind of fasting I have chosen: to loose the chains of injustice and untie the cords of the yoke, to set the oppressed free and break every yoke? Is it not to share your food with the hungry and to provide the poor wanderer with shelter?' (Isaiah 58.6–7). He cut that out too. The prophets were decimated and the Psalms, where God is the comfort of the afflicted, were ripped to pieces.

He got to the New Testament. Luke records Mary's wonderful song – her Magnificat. This poor Jewish peasant woman understood better than anybody else what the coming of Jesus meant. She said: 'He has brought down the rulers from their thrones but has lifted up the humble. He has filled the hungry with good things but has sent the rich away empty' (Luke 1.52–3). Mary doesn't sound like a social service provider in that text. She's speaking the language of social revolution. She's turning things upside-down. Then came Jesus' first sermon at

Nazareth, which I call his Nazareth Manifesto: 'The Spirit of the Lord is on me, because he has anointed me to preach good news to the poor' (Luke 4.18). Which is to say, if our gospel is the gospel of Jesus Christ – whatever else it is, whatever good it may do, however it may help us get over our drinking, save our marriages, or make us better people – whatever else it does, if it is not good news to poor people it is simply not the gospel of Jesus Christ.

Well, my friend snipped and snipped, and when he was through, that old Bible wouldn't hold together in my hands. It was a Bible full of holes, as opposed to a Holy Bible. I would take it out with me to preach, hold it high above American congregations and say: 'Brothers and sisters, this is our American Bible. It's full of holes from all the things we've ignored.' Once, our group of seminarians sat around in a circle and queried each other. We said: 'Out of all the sermons we have heard growing up in Bible-revering evangelical churches, how many have we heard about poverty?' None of us could remember ever hearing one sermon on this subject.

Authentic biblical faith

Thirty years ago they ran me off the ranch, as we would say, for talking this way about integrity. But now I'm welcomed at Trinity as a favourite son because there's a new generation of American evangelicals. I've now concluded that I was a nineteenth-century American evangelical, or an eighteenth-century British evangelical, born in the wrong century – a century full of a dualistic, privatized gospel according to which loving Jesus has nothing to do with loving justice.

But this sense of alienation goes back almost to my childhood. I grew up in the Plymouth Brethren Church, which broke off from the Church of England and moved to the US. As a teenager I began asking the elders in my church about racism in Detroit, where I lived. They told me that Christianity has nothing to do with racism. That issue is political, whereas the gospel is personal. These comments reflect the fact that for most of the twentieth century the American churches wandered in a wilderness caused by a schism between those who had a personal gospel and those who had a social gospel. The only place I found a real, holistic gospel was in the black churches.

My conversion text was Matthew 25, where Jesus says he was hungry, thirsty, a stranger, naked, sick, in jail and yet we never took care of him. The people say, 'Lord, when was it that we saw you hungry or thirsty or a stranger or naked or sick or in prison?' In effect, what they say is, 'Lord, we didn't know it was you. Had we known it was you, Lord, we would have done something, trust us, Lord. We would at least have formed a social action committee.'

We used to run a weekly food distribution centre near my home in Washington. Although only 20 blocks from the White House, in the capital city of the richest nation on earth, it's a neighbourhood in which the kids still go to bed at night to the sound of gunfire and where hundreds of people wait in line for a bag of groceries to get them through the week. Before the people came in, we would hold hands and say a prayer. An elderly Pentecostal woman named Mary Glover generally said the prayer, because she was our best pray-er. She would end with these words: 'Lord, we know that you'll be coming through this line today. So Lord, help us to treat you well.' That's a better commentary on Matthew 25 than all the scholars I've read!

A new generation of American evangelicals is discovering Charles Finney, the Billy Graham of the nineteenth century. He was a revivalist and an abolitionist. Although Billy Graham made the altar call famous around the world, it's thought that it was Finney who invented it. Finney had his converts come down the aisle because he wanted their names and addresses so he could sign them up for the anti-slavery cause. He preached the length and breadth of the United States and he talked about the kind of gospel that changed lives and neighbourhoods and nations, and could change social and political policy.

In the UK it was John Wesley. I learnt all I could about Wesley, and found I felt more at home in this tradition than in the twentieth-century evangelical world in which I was raised. It's not that all was bad in that world – it's just that it was so narrow, so constrained. It was the gospel squeezed into an American cultural mode. It didn't have liberating force and power. But when I began to read Wesley – his sermons and his journal – it all came alive to me.

Then I read about Wilberforce and the Clapham Sect. I went to Holy Trinity Church in Clapham, London, where this little group that was the engine of social reform went to church. The vicar showed me the table – he said, 'That's the table.' I said, 'What do you mean, "That's the table"?' It was a battered old table. He said, 'That's the table on which Wilberforce wrote the anti-slave trade legislation, and every Sunday we celebrate Holy Communion on it.' Slaves were freed and the Body and Blood of Christ are celebrated on the very same table. No more sacred–secular, no more political–personal, no more divisions. As followers of Jesus Christ, our concern is with all that is human.

The wind is changing. In the US we've begun something called 'Call to Renewal'. It's a kind of gang truce movement in the churches. The US churches have often been like gangs, with our turf, our territory, our grievances, our grudges and our paraphernalia. The vision for Call to Renewal came to me in 1993, during a gang Peace Summit we held in Chicago. All those who wanted to stop the violence and killing – including gang members of the Crips, Bloods, Vice Lords and Gangster Disciples – gathered together for three days. They asked a few of us who were religious leaders to come, because they said: 'We need spiritual power. We can't end the madness without it.'

On the last day of the gathering, Mac Charles Jones, a black Baptist preacher, did the sermon and then he did an altar call. A hundred and twenty-five gang leaders were interspersed throughout the regular congregation. They stood out because of their baggy pants, backwards baseball hats, tattoos and body armour. The sermon was on the parable of the Prodigal Son. A Jewish boy is in a far-off land, he's squandered his father's fortune, and he's in the hog pen. Eventually he comes to himself, gets up and goes home. He sees his father waiting, looking for him, and he begins to get his speech ready. 'Dad, I'm sorry, I messed up, I squandered the family inheritance, just make me one of your hired servants. I'd like to come home.' But he never even gets his speech out, because his father is so glad to see him. 'My son was lost, and now he's found. He was dead, and now he's alive. We're going to have a party.' So says the father, who of course in the story represents God. Now Mac looked like God standing there, 300 pounds of Baptist preacher. 'Get up out of the hog pen,' Mac boomed, 'come to yourself, come home, come home to the Church, the Church wants to have a party in your honour.'

Then came his altar call. Now, altar calls are a dangerous thing – how many verses of 'Just as I am' can you sing over and over again? We're on verse four, verse five, and nobody is moving. Finally, two young men get up and walk down the aisle. One is a Crip and one is a Blood. They're rival gang members. They've been trying to kill each other for a year in the drug war. They get in the pulpit, drop their gang colours and declare: 'From now on we walk the same road together.' There wasn't a dry eye in that church, but my tears came when I asked myself why, if the Crips and the Bloods can do this, the evangelicals and the liberals, the Catholics and the Protestants, the black and the white churches can't? We've been like gangs in the churches, and because of that our kids, especially those from the poorest backgrounds, have fallen between the cracks of our divisions.

My hope is that the churches can experience something similar to the Peace Summit through Call to Renewal – and now we've got all the gangs there. The Catholic bishops are there, the National Association of Evangelicals is there, the conservatives, and the National Council of Churches, the liberals – these two have been like Crips and Bloods for years. So we put a Mennonite between them, to make sure things go alright! But they're all there, and they're working on what Jesus said about those he called 'the least of these'. We don't agree on lots of other things, but we don't talk much about them. We talk about what it means that the gospel is good news for the poor.

The winds are changing, and not only in the US. In the UK, for instance, JustShare strikes me as a very hopeful initiative. But if you think this coalition of churches and agencies is only about social action, you're mistaken. If you think it's about politics, you're mistaken. It's about those things eventually, but it is about something more basic. It's about restoring the integrity of the word of God in our lives, our churches, our neighbourhoods, our workplaces and our nation. That is what this initiative is ultimately all about.

Spiritual drivers of change

I spend some of my spare time on an unusual hobby: reading biblical archaeology. I've learned that at certain periods of ancient Jewish history, excavations show that the houses were more or less the same size and the artefacts of life demonstrate a relative equality between the people. Interestingly, it is during those same periods that the prophets are silent. There are no prophetic words – no Amos, no Jeremiah, no Isaiah, no Micah. But when archaeologists dig down to layers relating to other periods of time, they find that there were great houses and small shacks, and the instruments of life show a great disparity between the people. It was at these times that the prophets rose up and thundered with the judgement and justice of God. And yet the disparities that prompted the prophets to speak out then would pale into insignificance compared to the disparities we accept as normal today.

The issue is not just poverty, it's inequality. Thirty years ago the gap in salary between the chief executive officer and average workers in US corporations was 30 to 1. It's about the same today in Japan and Germany. But in the US it's now 519 to 1. That would have made the prophets rage. Why doesn't it make us rage – where are the prophets of today?

This moment cries out for a social movement. History tells us that social movements with a spiritual foundation make the most difference. The US civil rights struggle was a movement guided by the strength and vitality of the black churches. Likewise, the abolitionist struggle wasn't just a movement against slavery. It was rooted in a spiritual revival, on both sides of the Atlantic. That's why I contend that the kind of globalization we face today will not change just by radical critique, or by saying, 'Look at the statistics, look at the facts, this is wrong. I am against this, I am a radical. I am going to protest.'

No, this movement needs an engine, a spiritual engine. It can't merely be about providing radical critique. It has to be about transformation – as Desmond Tutu would say, 'We need a spirituality for transformation.' It's encouraging that so many of the current social justice movements in the US have a spiritual base. There are movements about sweat shops, with college kids saying: 'We're not going to wear these clothes, or these running shoes any more, because they were made by exploited workers, women and kids most of all.' So they are challenging some big corporations, and Christian students are at the heart of this campaign. Jubilee 2000 started in the UK but it swept my country. Who would have thought it, when all the sceptics said: 'Governments don't forgive debts, banks don't forgive debts, prisons don't forgive debts'? But 26,000 petitions later, there was a movement in 60 countries. Bono and the Pope began to strategize, and all of a sudden we get debt cancellation. We're not done yet, but who would have thought we'd get this far in such a relatively short time?

We have a living wage campaign in my country. It says that people who work at the bottom ought to have a living wage. If you work hard full-time you shouldn't be poor. I teach at Harvard part-time, and we studied the living wage movement. Recently I got a call from one of my students. She said: 'I'm in the President's office at Harvard. Actually there's 40 of us here – we've sort of taken it over.' Harvard students occupied the President's office on behalf of food service employees, security guards and housekeepers, so they could earn a living wage. They risked their academic fortunes and futures, and they won. Campus Crusade for Christ was at the heart of that action, and so was Intervarsity Christian Fellowship. Movements like this in the US and around the world give me cause for great hope.

The UK Chancellor of the Exchequer, Gordon Brown, has gone on record as saying: 'Jubilee 2000 is the most important movement in Britain since Wilberforce and the slave trade.' It's a statement that reflects the fact that people are paying attention. Martin Luther King said that the Church is not the master or the servant of the state, but the conscience of the state.

The most important thing for this movement is not anger. There's lots of anger around, but ultimately that's not what makes movements grow. The most important thing is what we as people of faith are supposed to have an abundance of – the power and promise of hope. That's the most powerful contribution to social movements we can make. Hebrews says: 'Now faith is being sure of what we hope for and certain of what we do not see' (Hebrews 11.1). In my best paraphrase this reads:

'Hope is believing in spite of the evidence, and then seeing the evidence change.' That kind of hope can spark a movement and sustain it.

Somebody once asked Mark Twain what he thought about infant baptism. Why would anyone ask Twain, the great satirical essayist who was agnostic at best and probably an atheist at heart? But I love the response he gave. He said (if you'll excuse his language): 'Believe in it? Hell, I've seen it!'

Every time I speak these days, I say: 'I see a new movement for social and economic justice, being led in large part by people of faith.' People ask: 'But, Jim, how can you say that? We see concentrations of wealth and power, materialism, environmental degradation and inequality. How can you say you see a movement for justice, led by people of faith?' In reply I often quote Mark Twain, but as I'm an evangelical, I say: 'Believe it? Heck, I'm seeing it all over the place!'

Martin Luther King was part of a movement, and one of his top lieutenants, Vincent Harding, is my spiritual guide. He says: 'Jim, you can't start a movement, but you can prepare for one.' What we're doing now is getting ready for a movement. It's not here yet, but it will come in time. We're at the beginning of something that's going to grow and grow, because it is going to be a movement of faith. Finally, as Wesley and Martin Luther King and Desmond Tutu and so many others knew, there is no gospel that doesn't confront the world. In Jesus Christ, God hits the streets. That is at the core of our faith.

The last word goes to the prophets, for they have a vision for the global economy that can be our vision too. Listen to Isaiah:

Never again will there be in it an infant who lives but a few days, or an old man who does not live out his years . . . They will build houses and dwell in them; they will plant vineyards and eat their fruit. No longer will they build houses and others live in them, or plant and others eat. For as the days of a tree, so will be the days of my people; my chosen ones will long enjoy the works of their hands. They will not toil in vain or bear children doomed to misfortune; for they will be a people blessed by the Lord. (Isaiah 65.20–3)

So let us raise our voices with Amos:

'Let justice roll on like a river, righteousness like a never-failing stream!' (Amos 5.24)

Epilogue:
Towards a Sustainable Future

PETER HESLAM

There has been much discussion about the impact of the global economy on the environment in recent years. The stream of books, articles and conferences is unrelenting. There have been two major world summits on the issue. The first of these, held in Rio in 1992, was at the time the largest international conference ever to have been held, with over 25,000 delegates. It attracted great media attention and helped to raise public awareness of the issues. Ever since, political and business leaders have done a great deal to incorporate environmental concerns into their policies and actions. Evidence continues to mount, however, that many of the world's natural resources are under severe strain.

This raises a serious question. Can global capitalism ever ensure a sustainable environment? In other words, is sustainable global capitalism possible, or is it a contradiction in terms? This Epilogue is a brief reflection on this question from the perspective of the biblical story of creation. While the emphasis, inevitably, will be on global capitalism's darker sides, this is not intended to underestimate its benefits. On the contrary, key themes in the creation story, such as the celebration of freedom, abundance, the essential goodness of the material world, and the global scope of God's creative power, affirm all that is good in global capitalism. But when the challenges of economic globalization are considered, what are some of the economic implications of the following aspects of the creation story:

- having dominion?
- the creation of human beings in the image of God?
- the setting of certain limits in the created order?

Having dominion

We read in Genesis 1.26 that the first human beings were to 'have dominion' over the rest of creation. This passage has generally been interpreted in an anthropocentric way. It is often taken as licence for the extraction and manipulation of the earth's resources in the service of human 'needs'.[1] When Genesis 1 and 2 are taken together, however, it is clear that 'having dominion' is to be understood in terms of to 'till' and to 'keep' (Genesis 2.15), which are horticultural terms expressing nurture and care. This is what lies at the heart of the meaning of stewardship, and it provides the basis for a truly theocentric, ecological theology.

It also goes to the very heart of the original meaning of the term 'economics', derived from the Greek *oikonomia* – the responsible and careful administration of the household (*oikos*) of creation for the good of all. This is why Aristotle could claim that economics was part of ethics. It is also why Calvin insisted that markets are given by God not as a means of self-gratification but as a means of service. But this vision was largely lost under the impact of the Enlightenment, with its dualisms between the material and the spiritual, the real and the ideal. As a result, modern economics has tended to leave ethics out of its equations, preferring to see itself as a rational and objective science free from the partiality of moral commitment. Thus the term 'economic' tends now simply to mean 'financially profitable'. If a business, an investment, an industry is unprofitable, it is deemed 'uneconomic' and workers can be laid off and investments withdrawn. This is understandable because it all adds up on the balance sheet. In the process, however, economics is in danger of becoming a very narrow science.

Made in the image of God

Christians conclude from their reading of the Old and New Covenants that God is a trinity of persons-in-relation. It follows that if human beings are made in the image of God, then what is essential to human existence is being-in-relationship. In other words, human beings find their true identity in relationships, relationships that are characterized by intimacy and self-giving. This insight questions the way in which human beings are perceived in the process of economic globalization, which tends to be in terms of autonomous individuals. As such they are free from all obligation except that of serving their own self-interest. The fiercely competitive struggle to maximize returns through lowering production costs and dominating global markets is a key expression of this.[2]

The values of autonomy and competition can also be traced back to the Enlightenment, and find expression in the notions of 'the survival of the fittest' of evolutionary theory and of 'economic man' in classical and neo-classical economics. They have a dubious record, including monopolies of power, war, human degradation and environmental destruction.

Limits

Human beings, we read, were forbidden to eat the fruit from the tree of the knowledge of good and evil (Genesis 2.17; 3.1–3). They were also told to refrain from work on the sabbath because God rested from his work of creation on the seventh day (Exodus 20.8–11). Here, then, we have the notion of *rest* from economic activity, which suggests the value of restraint. Yet the emphasis on 'growth' and on 'choice', which are watchwords of the contemporary global economy, assumes that these are, or should be, unlimited. In a world in which both society and the environment are constrained by certain irremovable limits, it is not surprising that the unfettered pursuit of these objectives comes at a heavy human and environmental cost.

In search of a sustainable capitalism

Applying these insights of the creation story appears to leave little room for optimism as to whether global capitalism can ever be sustainable. The verdict of science is no more promising; many scientists claiming that if Western-style industrial development continues to be urged on the rest of the world, a few more planets besides this one would be needed to cope with the impact. No-one doubts the ability of the capitalist economy to muster and accumulate human-made capital on a vast scale. And few question the fact that it has helped to raise living standards for significant numbers of people. But there is growing recognition that as it does so, many of the natural resources on which economic prosperity depends are in rapid decline. There is a serious possibility, therefore, that global capitalism will eventually be dismantled by ecological forces.

It is, in fact, the limits of natural capital, rather than those of industrial and technological innovation, that are becoming the true limits to prosperity. The cheapness of the goods we consume shields us from this reality, because environmental costs are excluded from the production costs. What is critical here is not just the depletion of materials, such as fish, timber, oil and copper, but the loss of the service these resources supply in helping to sustain life. The exchange of carbon dioxide and oxygen, crucial for the continuance of nature, is a 'recycling service' provided daily free of charge for 6 billion people. The intensive burning of fossil fuels, however, means that the capacity of nature to recycle carbon dioxide is being exceeded – yet there is no known alternative to this recycling service.[3]

How can we begin to find a way out of this scenario? A good place to start is with the development of sustainable global capitalism, as a viable alternative to the dominant form of global capitalism we have today. For there is no inherent reason why it *has* to be a contradiction in terms. In the language of contemporary capitalism, the word 'capital' is generally used to refer to accumulated wealth in the form of investments, factories and equipment. To function properly, however, an economy needs four types of capital:

- human or 'social' capital (labour, skill, intelligence, culture and organization);
- financial capital (cash, investments and monetary instruments);
- manufactured capital (infrastructure, machines, tools and factories);

- natural capital (including not only natural resources but living systems and the services of the ecosystem).

The last of these, natural capital, is transformed by the industrial system's use of the first three – human, financial and manufactured capital – into the familiar objects of daily life: cars, roads, towns, bridges, houses, food, medicine, hospitals and schools. But in the process, the life-supporting capacity of natural capital is being eroded. What is needed, therefore, is a new kind of capitalism (if that is what we still want to call it) that places value on the largest stocks of capital it employs – the natural resources and living systems of natural capital and the social and cultural systems that are the basis of human capital. It would be a type of capitalism in which the fortunes of human, social and natural capital would take priority over the maximization of financial return. Without the setting of this priority, capitalism is not able to conform to its own accounting principles. Because its primary concern is with manufactured and financial capital, it can use up a good deal of its supplies of capital and yet can still record an increase in capital on its final balance sheet.

If capitalism is to become sustainable, so that future prosperity can be secured, there seems no other practical option – leaving aside any theological rationale – than that the use of natural capital needs to be made far more productive.[4]

The proposed manufacture of the hydrogen-powered fuel-cell car is an example of how this principle might work in practice. While recent advances in vehicle and fuel technology are bringing steady improvements, traditional cars contribute significantly to problems of local air quality, dependence on oil resources, and greenhouse gases. However, a simple reaction between oxygen from the air and hydrogen can be used to power vehicles with only pure water vapour as a local emission. Furthermore, hydrogen can be produced from a wide variety of primary energy sources, including renewable resources which do not contribute to greenhouse gas emissions. There is a long way to go before this approach becomes commercially viable, but already there are a number of pilot projects in operation. Research into this technology is in dire need of increased state funding and cross-industry collaboration, but as demand increases, the market will eventually underwrite the costs.

The fuel-cell car illustrates one of the basic assumptions of sustainable global capitalism: that, because of the absolute necessity of natural capital to economic prosperity, the interests of business and of the environment are not at odds with each other – or at least do not need to be. In other words, the economic not only ought not to be, but need not be, separated from the ecological and the social. Economic growth that damages ecology and society is ultimately *un*economic growth – growth that is unsustainable in the long term.

Conclusion

The biblical tradition does not provide us with a blueprint of how to run the economy. But reflection on only one of its themes – creation – provides a more than adequate framework within which the principles of sustainable global capitalism can begin to be developed. Indeed, it is encouraging to see the emergence of a number of non-governmental organizations, economic think-tanks and businesses addressing environmental and social concerns in ways that resonate deeply with the insights of the Judaeo-Christian faith. Contrary to the way they are often perceived, such groups are among those that represent the greatest hope for the future of global capitalism. By addressing issues of sustainability head-on and with rigour and imagination, they are helping to secure the prospects of business for decades to come. Indeed, there are good grounds for believing that the difficult choices that are now being made in business between sustainable and successful enterprise could one day become a distant memory. Sustainable global capitalism is global capitalism with a future.

Notes

1. See, for instance, Brian Griffiths, *Morality and the Market Place: Christian Alternatives to Capitalism and Socialism* (Hodder & Stoughton, London, 1982), pp. 79–80, and Richard Higginson, *Transforming Leadership: A Christian*

Approach to Management (SPCK, London, 1996), p. 7.

2. See The Group of Lisbon, *Limits to Competition* (MIT Press, Cambridge, MA, 1995).

3. I am particularly indebted to the book by Paul Hawken, Amory B. Lovins and L. Hunter Lovins, *Natural Capitalism: The Next Industrial Revolution* (Earthscan, London, 1999), for the formation of my views here.

4. For a fuller treatment of this point, see Peter S. Heslam, 'Sustainable Capitalism: A Contradiction in Terms?', in *Consumption, Christianity and Creation* (Sheffield Hallam University, Sheffield, 2002).

Index

The Capitalism Project DUE

The Capitalism Project at the London Institute for Contemporary Christianity (LICC) aims to develop a multi-disciplinary response to the theological, ethical, social and economic issues raised by globalization for business, governments, NGOs and individuals. It is involved not only in high-level teaching and research but also in developing resources for practitioners and non-specialists, including courses, study days and workshops.

The Project works in close association with a range of partners in business, finance, NGOs and churches. With organizations such as the Ridley Hall Foundation, the Jubilee Centre, the World Council of Churches and the Focolare Movement, it has run a number of conferences and seminars. It has also spearheaded the JustShare initiative, which involves a consortium of denominations and agencies, including Christian Aid and CAFOD, and seeks to explore issues of global economic justice around May Day. Together with Tearfund and World Vision it is working on a theology of development and on issues facing development workers.

London Institute for Contemporary Christianity

Founded in 1982 by John Stott, LICC's role is to equip Christians to engage biblically and vigorously with the issues they face in the contemporary world and to provide resources and materials across a wide range of issues. Directed by Mark Greene, its particular focus is on work, capitalism, media, gender issues, youth culture, communications, social trends, and skills in engaging with culture. Details of its faculty, courses and resources are available on its website or by contacting:

The London Institute for Contemporary Christianity
St Peter's
Vere Street
London W1G 0DQ
020-7399-9555
mail@licc.org.uk
www.licc.org.uk

The London Institute for
Contemporary Christianity